"I have a couple shelves full of books about expository preaching, all aimed, of course, at pastors. This is the first book I've ever read that offers insight and instruction for laypeople regarding how to listen to expository preaching. It's a superbly practical—and long overdue—handbook, covering the subject thoroughly yet clearly and concisely. Ken Ramey is a fine preacher and expositor himself with a shepherd's heart and a wonderful gift for teaching. I'm very grateful he has tackled this subject and given the church such an invaluable resource."

—JOHN MACARTHUR, pastor-teacher,
Grace Community Church, Sun Valley, CA

"I read Ken Ramey's book with pleasure and believe it should be distributed far and wide. It meets a neglected need in the life of the church. There cannot be enough emphasis placed upon the need for effective listening in the pew. Ramey proposes valuable solutions to the problem. He knows how to encourage people to listen to preaching by suggesting practical and helpful ways. The book is a valuable addition to the meager field of listening to sermons. I highly recommend it to every preacher, who would do himself and his congregation a huge favor by making it available. Get it today!"

—JAY ADAMS, author, *Be Careful How You Listen:
How to Get the Most Out of a Sermon*

"Good listening is missing today in all kinds of relationships, perhaps most of all in church. Many books have been written on how to preach well, but surprisingly, few have been published on how to listen well. Ken Ramey's *Expository Listening* admirably fills this void, from establishing a basic need for and theology of listening from the Scriptures to offering practical ways believers can prepare to listen, discern what they hear, and apply sermons to their own lives. I've been waiting for such a book for a long time. Christians everywhere should read it and put it into practice."

—JOEL R. BEEKE, president, Puritan Reformed
Theological Seminary, Grand Rapids, MI

"It is a powerful combination when a well-prepared preacher encounters a well-prepared congregation. Unfortunately, Christians often think it is the pastor alone who has an obligation to do any real preparation for the preaching event. The Bible has much to say to the contrary. I am grateful for Ken Ramey's urgent call for all Christians to heed scriptural instructions regarding how we are to embrace the exposition of His Word. *Expository Listening* is a much-needed handbook for this neglected aspect of church life. It is my hope that God will mightily transform many congregations as preachers *and listeners* take their biblical roles seriously."

—Dr. Michael Fabarez, senior pastor,
Compass Bible Church, Aliso Viejo, CA

"Nothing could be more important to the Christian life than skillful listening. Our God speaks. So it's vital that we hear and hear well. Hearing well involves absorbing the meaning of the speaker, in this case God. So Ken Ramey's thoughtful work in *Expository Listening* is nothing less than essential reading for all those who want to hear God speak and know the meaning of His Word. Take up this book, read, and listen."

—Thabiti Anyabwile, senior pastor, First Baptist
Church of Grand Cayman, Cayman Islands

"As Christians, we (rightly!) have high expectations of our pastors as they preach the Word of God. We expect that they will dedicate themselves to studying and understanding the Bible, that they will live lives marked by their commitment to holiness, that they will expend the effort necessary to craft gospel-centered, Spirit-empowered sermons. In short, we expect that they will come to the pulpit prepared, having dedicated themselves to the task they've been called to. How odd it is, then, that we are content to have such low standards for our own preparation? In this book, Ken Ramey shows that we ought to have equally high expectations of ourselves. For while the pastor preaches, we are to be attending to the Word, actively seeking to listen, to understand, to discern, to apply. Expository preaching demands expository listening. If you struggle to listen, if you struggle to know why you should listen, prayerfully read this book and heed its lessons."

—TIM CHALLIES, blogger, author,
www.discerningreader.com, Ontario, Canada

"Too often, churches are evaluated solely by how the pastor preaches. This is a place to start, but it is not the complete test. Of equal importance is how the people listen. With books on how to preach flourishing, how to listen to sermons is an area that has gone almost unnoticed, until now. Ken Ramey's *Expository Listening* is a guide for how to listen to and profit from faithful preaching of God's Word. It encourages the church attendee to move from being a passive member of an audience to being an active participant in the preaching and the worship of God, making *Expository Listening* a truly life-changing book. I know of nothing else like it."

—RICK HOLLAND, executive pastor, Grace
Community Church, Sun Valley, CA

Listening to a sermon is not like listening to the news, weather, and sports. And listening to a sermon well requires more than just paying attention. In *Expository Listening*, Ken Ramey will show you what the Bible says about listening well to God's Word preached, and he'll show you practical ways how to do it. Moreover, this book is not only valuable for individual reading, it can serve well as a group study.

—DONALD S. WHITNEY, associate professor of biblical spirituality,
Southern Baptist Theological Seminary, Louisville, KY

EXPOSITORY LISTENING

BY KEN RAMEY

KRESS
BIBLICAL
RESOURCES

Expository Listening
Published by Kress Biblical Resources
PO Box 132228
The Woodlands, TX 77393

Italics in Scripture quotations reflect the author's added emphasis.

ISBN 978-1-934952-09-2

Cover and interior design by Katherine Lloyd, (www.TheDESKonline.com)
Cover image by Jason Drumm

Published in the United States by Kress Biblical Resources.

Printed in the United States of America
2010—First Edition

10 9 8 7 6 5 4 3 2 1

To my beloved flock at Lakeside Bible Church,
who attentively listen to me preach the Word week after week
and prefer to have their toes stepped on rather than their ears tickled.

CONTENTS

FOREWORD

Have you ever arrived at church on Sunday in a less-than-ready condition for worship? Maybe you were up too late the night before, argued with your spouse while getting ready, possibly snapped at the kids, or even kicked the dog on the way out the door. By the time you get to church, you're not truly ready to listen to a sermon! But getting your mind and heart ready is exactly what expository listening requires.

Listening to a sermon, really listening—as in thinking, praying, following the argument, concentrating on the meaning and its application to your life—now that's hard work! Merely hearing a sermon is easy; it requires a properly functioning auditory system, but it's essentially a passive exercise. Actively listening to the preaching of God's Word requires mental alertness, focused attention, and a spiritually receptive heart. That's the kind of listening Solomon implored his own sons to do: "My son, if you will receive my words, and treasure my commandments within you, make your ear attentive to wisdom, incline your heart to understanding; for if you cry for discernment, lift your voice for understanding; if you seek her as silver, and search for her as for hidden treasures; then you will discern the fear of the LORD and discover the knowledge of God" (Prov. 2:1–5). That describes an exercise that's quite active, requiring energy and effort, and that's exactly what God would have us do each Sunday when we sit down in the pew for the purpose of engaging with Him. If the public proclamation of the Bible is the primary means of change in a believer's life (and it is: 1 Cor. 1:18; 1 Tim. 4:13; 2 Tim. 3:16–17), then it's vital that we get ourselves ready to listen to sermons from God's holy Word.

What I have argued for in the above paragraph is precisely why Dr. Ken Ramey's book, *Expository Listening: A Handbook for Hearing and Doing God's Word*, is so vital and necessary at this time for the body of Christ at large. Frankly, books on Christian preaching abound, while books on listening to Christian preaching are comparatively almost non-existent. It might be true to say that all the books dedicated to the sole purpose of teaching believers how to effectively listen to sermons that have ever been written could be counted on one hand. What you hold in your hands, therefore, is truly a particularly unique treatise.

I couldn't be more thrilled with what my friend Ken Ramey has done by showing the inseparable link between expository speaking and effective listening. The Christian church is indebted to him for what he teaches in this worthy volume. Now, as a result of our investment of time and effort in reading *Expository Listening: A Handbook for Hearing and Doing God's Word*, may we all serve this faithful expositor's Lord Jesus Christ—both his Savior and ours—by preaching and listening to God's glory.

Lance Quinn
Pastor-teacher, The Bible Church of Little Rock, Little Rock, AR
January 2010

ACKNOWLEDGMENTS

The Bible says to give honor to whom honor is due (Rom. 13:7). Therefore, it is appropriate for me to acknowledge those who have played a key role in the completion of this book. First of all, I am grateful for the faithful ministry of other men who have stimulated my thinking on the critical connection between preaching and listening, which has been almost completely ignored in the church today.

In 1991, Jay Adams addressed this colossal oversight in a book entitled *A Consumer's Guide to Preaching: How to Get the Most Out of a Sermon*. In the preface he stated:

> I have ransacked…libraries in several Christian institutions, looking through volumes on Christian living, spiritual growth, sermons, etc., trying to find what others have said about listening to sermons. There is virtually nothing but scraps—a passing comment here, an illustration there…. I have written this book because of the dearth of material devoted to the genuine concern for preaching from the listener's point of view. So far as I know, there is no other book like it.

Unfortunately, for various reasons, Adams's book never got the attention it deserved. However, it was recently rereleased in the spring of 2007 under a new title: *Be Careful How You Listen: How to Get the Most Out of a Sermon*. In the preface of the reprint he writes, "So little has been said or written about the obligation to listen well, that the subject is virtually unknown and untouched."

In other words, nothing has changed in sixteen years.

Ever since I was given a copy of the original edition of this relatively obscure book, it has held a treasured place on my shelf and in my mind. I am indebted to Adams for sensitizing me to this vital subject that has been flagrantly forgotten by the church today.

I must also give credit to my friend Lance Quinn, the pastor of The Bible Church of Little Rock, who wrote the epilogue to *Rediscovering Expository Preaching*, in which he briefly addressed "The Listener's Responsibilities." He insightfully concluded, "*Rediscovering Expository Preaching* would not be complete without a word about the listener's responsibilities in the expository process. Everything culminates in the hearers. The science and art of producing an expository sermon are empty efforts if no one hears and assimilates the message."

This book is my humble attempt to expand on this overlooked biblical theme of the listener's responsibility in preaching.

In the past couple years, I have come across a few excellent but brief Internet articles by some contemporary evangelical expositors such as Thabiti Anyabwile and Dr. Philip G. Ryken in which they seek to equip people to get the most out of a sermon. They address the issue of expository listening in a simple, straightforward way, for which I am grateful.

I recently acquired another DMin dissertation written in 1999 by Gene Curtis, a student at Gordon-Conwell Theological Seminary, entitled "How to Teach People to Listen More Effectively to the Preaching or Teaching of God's Word." His project was designed to provide pastors with a practical guide to motivate and equip the members of their congregation to be more effective hearers. He included several helpful tools that can be used in church settings to train members to develop practical listening skills (sermon outlines, a six-week small-group study guide, and a three-hour seminar). His kindred spirit to help people better understand their biblical responsibility as eager and active participants in the preaching event fueled my desire to take this subject one step further and write a book that appeals directly to church members and not just to pastors. At the same time, however, I hope this book will serve my fellow pastors by providing a practical resource that they can hand out to their congregations to complement their ministry of Bible exposition by helping their people better understand why they preach the way they do and how to get the most out of their expository sermons.

Toward the tail end of my research, I stumbled upon a gold mine in the bibliography of Joel Beeke's little book *The Family at Church: Listening to Sermons and Attending Prayer Meetings*. He included a number of original Puritan works that addressed the subject of listening to preaching. This was a major emphasis in the Puritans' ministries. They offered a good deal of practical direction to their congregations about how to properly listen to the preaching of God's Word and how to maximize its transforming power in their lives. Even though they have been dead for over three hundred years, I am indebted to them for their many insights on this matter.

I would be remiss if I didn't express my appreciation to Rick Holland, the director of DMin studies at The Master's Seminary for encouraging me to write on this subject; Rick Kress of Kress Biblical Resources for his eagerness to publish this book; along with my editor, Brian Thomasson, for the excellence and enthusiasm he applied to reorganizing and refining my original manuscript.

Finally, and most importantly, I want to acknowledge the ones who made the greatest sacrifice in the birthing of this book, my devoted wife, Kelli, and the three coolest kids on the planet, Zachariah, Hannah, and Jacob. I am a blessed man!

When we come to the Word preached, we come to a matter of the highest importance; therefore we should stir up ourselves and hear with the greatest devotion.

Thomas Watson

Introduction

WELCOMING THE WORD

"He who has ears to hear, let him hear."

MATTHEW 11:15

It is fascinating to observe how the evolution of church architecture throughout history visibly chronicles the devaluation of preaching. In past times, pulpits were erected high above the congregation, and the preacher literally had to climb a flight of stairs to stand behind the pulpit. The loftiness of the pulpit represented the authority of God's Word ruling over His people. Over time, the pulpit was brought down to stage level. Then it was moved off to the side in many cases to make room for the altar on which the sacraments were administered.

In more recent years, the historic sacred desk made of wood that symbolized the grandeur and gravity of preaching has been replaced with the more stylish, glitzy Plexiglas lectern. In some churches, pulpits have been removed to free up space for elaborate stage sets and musical productions. Besides, sitting on a stool promotes a much more casual, nonthreatening atmosphere for the speaker to share his thoughts and suggestions. Still others have gone so far as to seat their pastor on a couch alongside the congregation, thereby communicating a "hermeneutics of humility."

The high and lofty place of preaching has all but vanished from the contemporary church. Not only does the average churchgoer today no longer appreciate biblical preaching; they can't even tolerate it. Lax listeners, disinterested in hearing God's Word, have had their way, and people-pleasing pastors have all too readily complied. This should come as no surprise since the charge Paul gave to Timothy in 2 Timothy 4:1–2 regarding the preacher's obligation to faithfully preach the Word was explicitly given in view of the fact that a time was coming when people within the church "will not endure sound doctrine, but wanting to have their ears tickled, they will accumulate for themselves teachers in accordance to their own desires; and will turn away their ears from the truth and will turn aside to myths" (vv. 3–4). That time has come.

In stark contrast to this low estate stands Paul's testimony of the responsiveness of the first-century church in the port city of Thessalonica. The apostle Paul was immensely thankful for the manner in which they had received the preaching of God's Word (1 Thess. 2:13). During his brief ministry there, Paul experienced an unusual sense of the supernatural power of the Holy Spirit while he was preaching the gospel to them, and the Spirit of God used the Word of God to perform an amazing work in the their lives (1 Thess. 1:5). Virtually overnight, these idol-worshipping pagans were radically transformed into devoted followers of Jesus Christ (1:9).

What was the reason for all of this dramatic change? They had accepted his teaching "not as the word of men, but for what it really is, the word of God" (2:13). The word *accepted* was used to describe welcoming a guest into your home. The Thessalonians had swung the door of their hearts wide open and warmly embraced the Word as a cherished guest. They understood that by heartily welcoming the words of Paul's preaching, they were welcoming the authoritative counsel of God Himself into their hearts and lives.

So, how is your responsiveness to the Word of God?

Would Paul rave about you, like he did about the Thessalonian saints?

How are you at listening?

This book is unique in that it is about how to listen to the proclamation of the Bible, to preaching. While there have been countless books written for preachers on how to preach, only a handful of books and articles have been written to listeners on how to listen. Preachers have many resources to train and equip them to become better preachers, but listeners have hardly any resources to train and equip them to become better listeners.

This is astounding when you consider that the number of listeners far exceeds the number of preachers and even more so when you realize that the Bible says more about the listener's responsibility to hear and obey the Word of God than it does about the preacher's responsibility to explain and apply the Word of God. From cover to cover, the Bible is jam-packed with verses and passages that talk about the vital necessity of hearing and obeying God's Word. God is very concerned about how preachers preach. But based on the sheer amount of biblical references to hearing and listening, it is unmistakable that God is just as, if not more, concerned about how listeners listen.

A JOINT VENTURE

As a minister called by God to speak His Word, I am keenly aware of my inadequacy as a preacher to cause people's hearts to change, which makes me utterly dependent on the Holy Spirit to accomplish His work of transforming hearts and lives through the sermons I preach. I draw great comfort and confidence from the words of J. I. Packer, who said, "God's Spirit is sovereign. Through the Spirit's agency in both preacher and hearers, the Word of God becomes invincible. If fruitfulness depended finally on human wisdom and resourcefulness, no preacher would dare to speak a word, for no preacher ever feels…he has been wise and resourceful enough."[1]

While I am conscious of my limitations as a preacher, I am confident that the preaching of God's Word never returns void (Isa. 55:10–11). Yet in some sense, all the effort a preacher puts into preparing and delivering a sermon is useless if no one hears and obeys it. Preaching is not a one-sided endeavor. It is a joint venture between the preacher and the listener. Successful sermons result from the listener teaming up with the preacher much like a catcher works in unison with a pitcher. Both the pitcher and the catcher have an important role to play in the pitching process. The responsibility doesn't all rest on the pitcher's shoulders. Likewise, the responsibility in preaching doesn't all rest on the preacher's shoulders. The listener plays a vital role in the preaching process.

In order for you to receive the maximum benefit from the sermons you hear, you must partner with the preacher so that the Word of God accomplishes its intended purpose of transforming your life. Nothing creates a more explosive, electrifying, life-changing atmosphere than when the lightning bolts from a Spirit-empowered preacher hit the lightning rods of a Spirit-illuminated listener. George Whitfield, one of the most dynamic preachers of all time, once said, "If only all who hear me this day would seriously apply their hearts to practice what has now been told them! How ministers would see Satan, like lightning, fall from heaven, and people find the Word preached sharper than a two-edged sword and mighty, through God, to the pulling down of the devil's strongholds!"[4]

There is no telling the dynamic impact the Spirit of God will make through the Word of God any time someone who faithfully explains and applies God's Word comes in contact with someone who faithfully listens to and obeys God's Word.

This powerful synergy that makes the Word of God "invincible" and causes the proclaimers of the Word to fall over backwards with gratitude at the responsiveness of the listeners is what this book is all about. The Thessalonians knew it wasn't Paul talking; it was God talking. Paul had no qualms about claiming to speak for God. Neither did the apostle Peter. He admonished those with the gift of preaching/teaching, saying: "Whoever speaks, is to do so as one who is speaking the utterances of God" (1 Pet. 4:11). In fact, all the apostles and prophets, including Jesus Himself, viewed themselves as God's mouthpieces, whose sacred duty was to boldly speak on God's behalf (Jer. 1:9; 5:14; John 14:24; 2 Cor. 5:20). The very word *preach* (Greek *keruxon*) means to "proclaim as a herald." In biblical times, kings and rulers had special heralds who made announcements to the people on their behalf. They served as ambassadors whose job was to speak for the king and tell the people exactly what he told them to say.

As a representative of the King of kings, preachers have been given the responsibility and authority to boldly herald forth what God has said in His Word. But the hearers have a responsibility too, one that's equally pressing: They must engage themselves as wholehearted, blood-earnest listeners who respond to the call of God on all humankind: "Listen, O heavens, and hear, O earth; for the LORD speaks" (Isa. 1:2).

In the pages ahead, we will explore God's call to listen. We'll begin by covering a broad theology of listening, a biblical audiology. Once that foundation is laid, we will begin to look at how all this highfalutin theology must work itself out in your heart, your mind, and your life. After all, if you are like most Christians, you listen to at least one or two sermons a week. Let's say you came to Christ at age ten and you live to be seventy-five. If you average two sermons a week, you will listen to over seven thousand sermons during the course of your life. And at end of your life you will stand before God and give an account for every sermon you heard. On that day, God will essentially ask you, "How has your life changed as a result of the thousands of times you have heard My Word preached?" So we see that it is vital that you are ever welcoming the Word of God and diligently seeking to put what you hear into practice, thus proving "yourselves doers of the word, and not merely hearers who delude themselves" (James 1:22).

A PLEA FOR LISTENERS

Those who take to heart God's call to listen will transcend the discouraging trends in the church today. All around us, clear, convicting, authoritative preaching straight from God's Word is being devalued by both those standing in the pulpit and those sitting in the pew.

The church growth movement that boomed during the eighties and nineties concluded that preaching is an outdated form of communication in our technologically advanced, media-savvy society. Surveys found that most listeners were interested only in hearing amusing and inspiring messages that addressed the practical problems they face in life (relating to your spouse, raising kids, surviving the rat race, battling addictions, etc.).

In the last few years, the Emergent Church Movement has undermined biblical preaching even further by declaring that people no longer recognize the authority of propositional truth or the authority of the preacher. Consequently, preachers must be less authoritative, add more dialogue—swap out biblical confrontation for mere conversation. In fact, some in the movement have gone so far as to hold that the traditional form of preaching characterized by bold declaration is detrimental to the church.[2] Apparently, even the use of a PA system has become unhelpful because it "creates the situation where the recipients are powerless to speak back. What makes this situation even more insidious is when the person with the power of the microphone is also the person who is presuming to speak for God."[3] But isn't that precisely the situation the church was designed to create—a dynamic duo of faithful herald and fervent listeners?

The Thessalonians understood this supernatural dynamic and it caused them to have a great appreciation and affection for the preached Word. They loved to listen to Paul preach. They could be truly described as preaching enthusiasts, preaching fanatics even. Augustine urged his congregation to attend preaching with "burning thirst and fervent hearts."[5] Likewise, the Puritans, as we will see throughout this book, understood this dynamic of biblical exposition—that when a man is faithfully preaching the Word of God it is actually the voice of God being heard—which should cause you to pay earnest attention to every sermon you hear. From the very first Sunday I began preaching expository sermons to the congregation God has called me to shepherd, I have sought to develop in congregants a robust appetite and a real appreciation for preaching that comes straight from the Bible, along with an uncompromising commitment to do whatever the Bible says. By and large, they know that "congregations never honor God more than by reverently listening to His Word with a full purpose of praising and obeying Him once they see what He has done and is doing, and what they are called to do."[6] My desire within these pages is to create congregations that share this passion to honor God by being discerning hearers of His Word, diligent doers of His Word, and devoted lovers of His Word, preaching fanatics, even, who come to church like a thirsty man craving something to drink and whose hearts fervently long to hear the Word preached because they know that in it God speaks to them.

Hearing is the provision made for the soul's eternal well-being, its everlasting welfare depends on it; if you fail here, your souls perish without remedy. For salvation comes by faith and faith comes by hearing. It is an act of eternal consequence. According to our hearing, so shall the state of our souls be to eternity.

David Clarkson

One

BIBLICAL AUDIOLOGY: A THEOLOGY OF LISTENING

For "whoever will call on the Lord will be saved." How then will they call on Him in whom they have not believed? How will they believe in Him whom they have not heard? And how will they hear without a preacher? How will they preach unless they are sent? Just as it is written, "How beautiful are the feet of those who bring good news!" However, they did not all heed the good news; for Isaiah says, "Lord, who has believed our report?" So faith comes from hearing, and hearing by the word of Christ.

ROMANS 10:13–17

Hearing is a precious thing. The apostle Paul says hearing is required for us even to have faith. Faith comes from hearing. Hearing is not enough though. There's also heeding—and not all of those who hear heed. That is to say, even if the trillions of tiny pulsations of air pressure reach the unimaginably intricate machinery in your inner ear, where they are inexplicably translated into words that form ideas in your brain, you might not actually listen. You might choose to do nothing with the information. In fact, there may be any number of problems with your hearing. It could be that you simply lack the

9

discernment to know whether or not you are listening to biblical preaching. Perhaps you are listening to preaching you would do best to ignore. Perhaps you have sought out preaching that only makes you feel better about yourself. Or perhaps the preaching is good, but you are the problem. You are burned out on listening. It seems like all you do is listen, while experiencing little growth and change in your life. Week after week, good sermons go in one ear and out the other without ever penetrating your mind or piercing your heart and transforming your life. Perhaps you have the discernment and the desire to obey, but you're listening to and watching so much during the week that's not important or entirely accurate that you've trained yourself to only half listen, a habit you can't seem to "turn off" on Sunday mornings. All these hearing problems are the result of never being trained to properly appreciate and practically appropriate God's Word.

We are in desperate need of both theological and practical instruction in the area of listening effectively to the preaching of the Word. Becoming a better listener begins by establishing a basic theology of listening, a biblical audiology.[1] This should be simple enough to formulate, as listening is a dominant theme in Scripture. Almost every book of the Bible contains some reference to hearing and obeying God's Word. From Genesis to Revelation—through the poets and prophets in the Old Testament and through Christ and the apostles in the New Testament—God beckons us to hear and heed Him. The God of the Bible commands us to listen to what He has said, and He threatens punishment if we don't, while promising blessing if we do. The pattern is pretty difficult to miss: It goes: command, threat, promise. And in between, there are examples, narratives describing those who endeavored to obey God—Enoch, Abraham, Stephen—and those who chose not to—Adam, Pharaoh, Judas.

We might systematize everything the Bible teaches on the subject of listening by arranging the verses under four summary statements, or theological truths, as follows:

1. God has spoken and commands us to listen to and obey what He has said.
2. We all fail to listen to and obey God and deserve to be punished by Him.
3. God grants us the ability to listen to and obey Him by His Holy Spirit, whom we receive through faith in Jesus Christ.
4. God promises to bless us both now and for all eternity if we listen to and obey Him.

Notice how each of these statements is related to several other key theological themes in Scripture. The first statement relates to the nature of God and His Word. The second statement relates to the nature of man and sin. The third statement relates to the nature of salvation, the Holy Spirit, and Jesus Christ. And the fourth statement relates to sanctification and future things. So the theology of listening overlaps and intermingles with virtually every aspect of systematic theology. It's almost as if the theology of listening comprises an entire catechism or statement of faith!

Let's look at these four theological statements about listening one at a time.

1. God has spoken and commands us to listen to and obey what He has said.

Motivated by a desire to have a relationship with humankind through which He could display His glory, God, the creator and sustainer of the universe, gave us His Word, the Bible, to reveal to us what we need to know and do in order to have a relationship with Him. Over a period of fifteen hundred years (1400 BC–AD 90), God chose approximately forty men through whom He spoke. The book of Hebrews begins with these words: "God, after He spoke long ago to the fathers in the prophets and in many portions and in many ways, in these last days has spoken to us in His Son" (1:1–2). Under the supervision of His Spirit, men like Job, Moses, Joshua, Samuel, Ezra, Nehemiah, David, Solomon, Isaiah, Jeremiah, Daniel, Matthew, Mark, Luke, John, Peter, and Paul wrote down word for word everything God wanted us to know and do. Peter said, "But know this first of all, that no prophecy of Scripture is a matter one's own interpretation [i.e. origination], for no prophecy was ever made by an act of human will, but men moved by the Holy Spirit spoke from God" (2 Pet. 1:20–21).

This process God used to "breathe out" His Word to humankind is referred to as the verbal, plenary inspiration of Scripture (2 Tim. 3:16–17). What that means is that each and every word in the Bible is exactly what God wanted said. In other words, the Bible is the very words of God and therefore absolutely true and reliable. Since God has spoken and His words have been accurately recorded and safely preserved within the pages of Scripture, we can affirm with confidence that "when the Bible speaks, God speaks!"[2]

This also means when a preacher faithfully preaches the Bible, it is God speaking and not the preacher (John 14:24; Acts 13:7, 44). By virtue of the fact that God is the one who spoke it, we should listen and obey.

It's *His* Word.

Just like a child should listen to and obey what their parents say for no other reason than it is the right thing to do because of who they are (Eph. 6:1–2), we should listen to and obey what our heavenly Father has said because of who He is. God's Word is an expression of all that He is. He spoke forth His Word so that we would know about His glory, His love, His grace, His mercy, His power, His wrath, His justice, His goodness, His faithfulness, etc. God's character is inherent in His Word (cf. Ps. 138:2). What makes the Bible so dynamic and gives it the ability to dissect our hearts with such precision and so accurately discern every aspect of our lives is because it is the Word of the all-powerful, all-knowing God (Heb. 4:12–13). Whenever we are exposed to the Word of God we are in essence being exposed to God Himself (1 Cor. 14:24–25). That alone should be enough to motivate us to honor and obey the Word of God.

This was the conviction of those called by God to preach in both the Old and New Testaments. Often times the first words out of their mouth were "Thus says the Lord!" or "Hear the word of the Lord!" It was through these mouthpieces that God not only spoke to us, but also commanded us to listen and obey.

Note just a few of the many commands throughout the Bible to listen and obey:[3]

"Hear, O Israel, the statutes and ordinances which I am speaking today in your hearing, that you may learn them and observe them carefully." (Deut. 5:1)

"Hear, O My people, and I will admonish you; O Israel, if you would listen to Me!... Oh that My people would listen to Me, that Israel would walk in My ways." (Ps. 81:8, 13)

Behold, a voice out of the cloud, saying, "This is My beloved Son, with whom I am well-pleased; listen to Him." (Matt. 17:5)

Everywhere, the Bible asserts the fact that it is the unchanging, everlasting, life-giving, life-changing Word of God and that we would do well to listen to it (Isa. 40:5, 8; 51:4; 55:10–11; Jer. 23:29; Heb. 4:12). In fact, how well our life goes and how well it ends up is determined by how well we listen to and obey the Word of God. God told Israel that their spiritual survival was at stake based on whether or not they did what He told them. Deuteronomy 6:24 says, "So the LORD commanded us to observe all these statutes, to fear the LORD our God for our good always and our survival." Several times, God told Israel that listening to and obeying His Word was a matter of life and death for them (4:1; 8:3). In Deuteronomy 30:19–20, Moses said, "I have set before you life and death, the blessing and the curse. So choose life in order that you may live, you and your descendants, by loving the LORD your God, by obeying His voice, and by holding fast to Him; for this is your life and the length of your days." Helping the people of God make the vital connection between obedience to His words and the satisfaction of life in God's world was a key element of Moses' ministry to them. After all, "man does not live by bread alone, but man lives by everything that proceeds out of the mouth of the LORD" (8:3).

But God extends His Word and His call to obedience even beyond His own chosen people. He calls out to all humankind, as only one with the authority of a sovereign creator could: "Listen carefully to Me, and eat what is good, and delight yourself in abundance. Incline your ear and come to Me. Listen, that you may live" (Isa. 55:2–3). Only God can guarantee the good results of obeying His own commands. Jesus extended the blessing of obedient listening to eternity, saying, "Truly, truly, I say to you, he who hears My word, and believes Him who sent Me, has eternal life, and does not come into judgment, but has passed out of death into life. Truly, truly, I say to you, an hour is coming and now is, when the dead shall hear the voice of the Son of God; and those who hear shall live" (John 5:24–25). Later He said, "The words that I have spoken to you are spirit and are life" (6:63). When Jesus asked the disciples if they were going to withdraw from Him like so many others had, Peter replied, "Lord, to whom shall we go? For you have words of eternal life" (v. 68).

Listening to and obeying God is the key to establishing and maintaining a relationship with Him that results in an abundant life now and eternal life spent with Him in heaven. But the problem is that none of us comes close to listening to and obeying God in the way He commands.

2. We all fail to listen to and obey God and deserve to be punished by Him.

From the beginning, humankind has failed to listen to and obey what God has said. Adam and Eve disobeyed the very first words God ever spoke to man. God created Adam and Eve and placed them in the Garden of Eden and clearly told them what to do and what not to do: "And the LORD God commanded the man, saying, 'From any tree of the garden you may eat freely; but from the tree of the knowledge of good and evil

you shall not eat, for in the day that you eat from it you shall surely die"
(Gen. 2:16–17). But along came Satan and bent the ear of Eve, who chose
to listen to what he said instead of what God had said (3:1–6). Adam and
Eve's disobedience caused a spiritual separation in their relationship with
God. As a result, God cursed them and banished them from the Garden.

How ironic, how tragic, that the pinnacle of God's creation does not
heed Him from His first words! The original sin resulted from a failure to
listen to and obey what God had said. Ever since then, every person who
has ever lived has been corrupted by sin and separated from God (Rom.
5:12). We are all born with a sin nature that renders us spiritually dead
and therefore incapable of hearing (Ps. 51:5; Eph. 2:1–3). A dead man
can't hear anything. In describing the sinfulness of humankind, David
wrote: "The wicked are estranged from the womb; these who speak lies
go astray from birth. They have venom like the venom of a serpent; like a
deaf cobra that stops up its ears, so that it does not hear the voice of the
charmers, or a skillful caster of spells" (Ps. 58:3–5).

We are all by nature alienated from God and hearing impaired.
Puritan Thomas Shepard wrote, "From that great distance and infinite
separation of men's souls from God…though God calls…they cannot
hear no more than men a thousand miles off."[4] The doctrine of total
depravity, better referred to as inability, leads us to the conclusion that all
of our faculties have been ruined by sin—from our ability to think and
reason right down to our ability to hear. We don't want to listen to God,
and besides, we can't. Romans 8:7–8 says, "The mind set on the flesh is
hostile toward God; for it does not subject itself the law of God, for it
is not even able to do so; and those who are in the flesh cannot please
God." We are all naturally antagonistic to God's Word. Our sinful rebellion makes us stubborn and unwilling to listen to God. We don't want
anything to do with Him, and even if we did, it is impossible in and of
ourselves to comprehend what God has said.

And it's not just that we have a hard time paying attention to God.
One of the most basic effects of the Fall is our inability to understand,

let alone do, what God has said. Jesus said, "Why do you not understand what I am saying? It is because you cannot hear My Word.... He who is of God hears the words of God; for this reason you do not hear them, because you are not of God" (John 8:43, 47). Paul affirmed natural man's inability to comprehend the Word of God: "There is no one who understands, there is no one who seeks for God" (Rom. 3:11). All men are "darkened in their understanding" (Eph. 4:18). "The word of the cross is foolishness to those who are perishing" (1 Cor. 1:18). In other words, the gospel message doesn't make any sense to those who remain in their natural sinful state. The reason is, "a natural man does not accept the things of the Spirit of God; for they are foolishness to him, and he cannot understand them" (2:14). The Spirit of God is the one who enables us to hear and understand what God has said in His Word.

We are all born without this key component that allows us to hear God's Word. It's as if we have been wired with an AM receiver, but God is broadcasting on FM. Without the indwelling and illuminating presence of the Holy Spirit in our lives, all we are able to pick up is static. That's why the Bible and preaching do not make sense to unbelievers. All it does is puzzle them, bore them, or infuriate them. At the same time, however, even believers who have the Holy Spirit within them still struggle with what one of my seminary professors called "a hamartiological hangover." Based on the record of Scripture, God's people are the worst culprits when it comes to not listening to and obeying His Word.

Consider some of the Old Testament examples of those who failed to listen to and obey God's Word:[5]

> For the sons of Israel walked forty years in the wilderness, until all the nation, that is, the men of war who came out of Egypt, perished because they did not listen to the voice of the LORD, to whom the LORD had sworn that He would not let them see the land which the LORD had sworn to their fathers to give us. (Josh. 5:6)

"Go, inquire of the LORD for me and the people and all Judah concerning the words of this book that has been found, for great is the wrath of the LORD that burns against us, because our fathers have not listened to the words of this book, to do according to all that is written concerning us." (2 Kings 22:13)

"To whom shall I speak and give warning that they may hear? Behold, their ears are closed and they cannot listen. Behold, the word of the LORD has become a reproach to them; they have no delight in it…. I set watchmen over you, saying, 'Listen to the sound of the trumpet!' But they said, 'We will not listen.'" (Jer. 6:10, 17)

The entire Old Testament is one long, sad commentary on God's desire to be heard and the failure of His people to listen. In summarizing the history of the nation of Israel, "one might almost say that the epitaph engraved on the nation's tombstone was: 'The Lord God spoke to his people, but they refused to listen.'"[6] The nation of Israel is a tragic example of what happens when people fail to listen to God's Word. They were stubborn and stiff-necked and refused to use the ears God had given them. As a result, God made good on His countless threats to punish them:[7]

"Like the nations that the LORD makes to perish before you, so you shall perish; because you would not listen to the voice of the LORD your God." (Deut. 8:20)

"If you will not listen to the voice of the LORD, but rebel against the command of the LORD, then the hand of the LORD will be against you, as it was against your fathers." (1 Sam. 12:15)

"So I will choose their punishments and will bring on them what they dread because I called, but no one answered; I spoke, but they did not listen." (Isa. 66:4)

In the New Testament, Jesus threatened similar judgment to those who refused to listen to His words and obey what He said. He likened them to a man who built his house on the sand and a violent storm destroyed it completely (Matt. 7:24–27; Luke 6:46–49). That's what will happen to everyone who doesn't hear and obey the words of Christ. On the Judgment Day, when God's wrath sweeps across the earth, their lives will be obliterated and their souls will experience eternal separation from God. Hell is filled with people who wish they had listened and obeyed. Consider a few New Testament examples of people who failed to listen to and obey God's Word:[8]

> "Therefore I speak to them in parables; because while seeing they do not see, and while hearing they do not hear, nor do they understand." (Matt. 13:13)

> He answered them, "I told you already and you did not listen; why do you want to hear it again? You do not want to become His disciples too, do you?" (John 9:27)

> Concerning him we have much to say, and it is hard to explain, since you have become dull of hearing. (Heb. 5:11)

Listening to God is such a basic requirement for life in His universe that it's astonishing that humankind cannot seem to comply. The prophet Isaiah expressed our Creator's lament at this: "Sons I have reared and brought up, but they have revolted against Me. An ox knows its owner, and a donkey its master's manger, but Israel does not know, My people do not understand" (Isa. 1:2–3). The beasts of burden acquiesce to their masters, but the very sons revolt. It's no wonder that God's patience will not last forever. The eventual punishment for not listening to God is God not listening to us. God threatens that if we don't listen to Him, there may come a day when He will no longer listen to us (Deut. 1:43–45;

Prov. 28:9; Jer. 11:14; Zech. 7:13). Perhaps there is no greater incentive to listen to and obey the Word of God than this.

3. God grants us the ability to listen to and obey Him by His Holy Spirit, whom we receive through faith in Jesus Christ.

We are all horrible hearers who, as a result of the Fall, have been rendered incapable of understanding and obeying what God has said in His Word. It is impossible for us to comprehend and comply with God's Word without the help of the Holy Spirit (1 Cor. 2:11–14). The Spirit of God is integral to accepting and applying the Word of God. That's why it is imperative that we understand the regenerating and illuminating work of the Holy Spirit.

In order to be able to hear and heed God's Word, we must first be regenerated by the Holy Spirit. Jesus likened the process of regeneration to being reborn, not physically, but spiritually (John 3:3–8). Being born again is a supernatural act of the Spirit of God whereby He grants spiritual life to those who are dead in sin and transforms them into a totally new person (Eph. 2:1–6). The tool the Holy Spirit uses to bring spiritually dead people to life is the Word of God (Eph. 1:13; 6:17, James 1:18, 1 Pet. 1:23). A person is regenerated when the Holy Spirit convicts them of their sin and convinces them that they must be clothed in the righteousness of Jesus Christ in order to escape the coming judgment of God (John 16:8). The moment a person is born again, the Holy Spirit gives them a new nature, which is evident by the transformation that takes place in their life (Rom. 12:2; Eph. 4:22–24; Titus 3:5).

One of the clearest evidences that a person truly has been born again is a love for God's Word. Before the Spirit regenerates us, we are baffled and bored by preaching. But once we are saved, it suddenly makes sense to us and becomes interesting and begins to have a transforming effect on our lives. There are people attending churches all across this world who have gone to church their entire lives but have little or no interest in the preaching of God's Word. That is evidence that they have never truly been born again. They may have made a profession of faith in Christ, but they don't truly know Him as their Lord and Savior. Knowing Jesus Christ is the indispensable prerequisite for being able to receive and respond to what God has said in His Word. Jesus Himself said, "My mother and My brothers are these who hear the word of God and do it" (Luke 8:21). To Jesus, there can be no mistaking them. Jesus said to the religious leaders of His day, "I know that you are Abraham's descendants; yet you seek to kill Me, because My word has no place in you" (John 8:37). In the same context he said, "He who is of God hears the words of God; for this reason you do not hear them, because you are not of God" (8:47). So in order to be "of God" and hear and obey "the Word of God" we must be born again (John 18:37; 1 Thess. 2:13; Heb. 4:2; 1 John. 4:5-6).

After regenerating us, the Spirit of God takes up residence within us. Before Jesus returned to heaven, He promised to send the Holy Spirit to help His followers learn and live out His words (John 14:16; 16:12–15; 1 John 2:27). It is the abiding presence of the Holy Spirit that causes us not only to want to hear the truth of God's Word but also to be able to grasp it and do it. This ongoing work of the Holy Spirit in the life of every believer is called *illumination*. Illumination is the ministry of the Holy Spirit whereby He enlightens believers, enabling them to understand and apply the Word to their life.

The moment we are born again, it's as if we are given a new set of hearing aids or a new pair of glasses that enable us to hear and see in God's Word what we couldn't before. From then on, not only are we able to comprehend what God has said, but the Holy Spirit who now indwells us also convicts us about what God's Word says and convinces us of it, as well as conforming our lives to it. That's why whenever we are exposed to the Word of God, we need to remember to ask the Spirit to illumine our minds and hearts so that we understand what it means and how it applies. Who better to ask to help us accurately interpret and practically implement the Word than the one who inspired it in the first place?

So we can't hear and obey the Word of God without the regenerating and illuminating ministry of the Holy Spirit. Remarkably, we don't receive the Holy Spirit until we receive Jesus Christ, and we can't receive Jesus Christ unless we receive the Word of God, and we won't receive the Word of God unless the Holy Spirit opens up our ears to hear. God made our ears, and He opens and closes them as He pleases (Exod. 4:11; Prov. 20:12; Deut. 29:4; Job 33:16; 36:10–12, 15; Ps. 40:6; Mark 7:37; Rom. 11:8). So while it's true that our ability to hear the word of Christ is the link between the revelation of God and the salvation of your soul, it's equally true that we are completely dependent on God's sovereignty for the outcome. Sometimes God sends forth His Word for the purpose of hardening and damning people rather than softening, saving, and sanctifying them (Isa. 55:10–11; 2 Cor. 2:15–17). That's why we must urgently cry out to Him to open our ears so we can hear and heed His Word (Isa. 50:4–5), particularly in light of the fact that our very life and eternal destiny hinge on it.

4. God promises to bless us both now and for all eternity if we listen to and obey Him.

As I mentioned earlier, how we respond to what God has said in the Bible is what ultimately determines the kind of life we live here on earth and where we will spend eternity. Listening to and obeying God is the key to experiencing abundant life now and spending eternity with Him in heaven. Not listening to and obeying Him results in having to live a life without His help and hope and then being separated from Him forever in hell. Consider just a few of the many promises in the Bible to those who listen and obey:[9]

> "It shall come about, if you listen obediently to my commandments which I am commanding you today, to love the LORD your God and to serve Him with all your heart and all your soul, that He will give the rain for your land in its season, the

early and late rain, that you may gather in your grain and your
new wine and your oil. He will give grass in your fields for your
cattle, and you will eat and be satisfied." (Deut. 11:13–15)

"But he who listens to me shall live securely and will be at ease
from the dread of evil." (Prov. 1:33)

"Blessed are those who hear the word of God and observe it."
(Luke 11:28)

There you have it—a biblical audiology. These four principles form
a theological foundation of listening on which the rest of the practical
instruction in this book is built. As we move forward, I will seek to help
you diagnose and treat your listening problems. The first and most critical area we must address is, of course, your heart, for "from it flow the
springs of life" (Prov. 4:23). It could be that your listening problem is a
heart problem after all.

FOR STUDY OR DISCUSSION

1. Out of the overwhelming number of biblical references to
   listening/hearing and obeying, which are the most com-
   pelling: the commands, the threats, the promises, or the
   examples? Why?
2. Read Psalm 58:3–5; John 8:43, 47; Romans 3:11; 8:7–8;
   1 Corinthians 1:18; 2:14. How has total depravity affected
   your ability to hear and obey God's Word?
3. Read Deuteronomy 8:3; 30:19–20; Isaiah 55:2–3; John 5:24–
   25; 6:63, 68. What is the connection in these verses between
   listening and your life here on earth, as well as your eternal
   destiny?

*Thank God for graciously opening your ears
so you could hear and obey His Word
and have a relationship with Him.
Ask Him to help you learn to listen
like your life depends on it.*

Come not to hear with a careless heart, as if you were to hear a matter that little concerned you, but come with a sense of the unspeakable weight, necessity, and consequence of the holy word which you are to hear: and when you understand how much you are concerned in it, and truly love it, as the word of life, it will greatly help your understanding of every particular truth. That which a man loveth not, and perceiveth no necessity of, he will hear with so little regard and heed, that it will make no considerable impression on his mind.

Richard Baxter

Two

HEARING WITH YOUR HEART

"The sower went out to sow his seed; and as he sowed, some fell beside the road, and it was trampled under foot and the birds of the air ate it up. Other seed fell on rocky soil, and as soon as it grew up, it withered away, because it had no moisture. Other seed fell among the thorns; and the thorns grew up with it and choked it out. Other seed fell into the good soil, and grew up, and produced a crop a hundred times as great...."

LUKE 8:5–8

The first church I pastored was a twenty-first-century version of the Parable of the Soils. I was warned on my initial visit that I was likely going to have a fight on my hands, which obviously made me leery of taking the position. In order to encourage me and alleviate my fear of walking into a potential hornet's nest, one of the guys on the search committee e-mailed me and said, "Paul's pattern was to go into a city, start a riot, and go to jail. We'll try to keep you out of jail!" Well, I went and sure enough, it didn't take long for a riot to break out in the church. One of the first indicators that the church was heading for a train wreck was the conflicting responses I got to my sermons.

I'll never forget one Sunday, when I was standing by the back door greeting people as they left. Someone came up to me and enthusiastically reached out and grabbed my hand and said, "That was the best sermon I have ever heard!" At that very same moment, out of the corner of my eye, I noticed a group of disgruntled folks huddled in the corner of the foyer, who, according to what was reported to me later, were discussing how that was "the worst sermon they had ever heard!"

As the church became more and more polarized in the following months, that particular incident provided me with the comfort and confidence I needed to persevere through those challenging times. It was that diametrically opposite response to the preaching of God's Word that allowed me to maintain a proper perspective as to what was really going on, not so much in the church, but in people's hearts. As I continued to faithfully throw out the seed of the Word of God, it landed on different types of soils and produced various responses. Some openly rejected it; others merely put up with it; while others couldn't get enough of it.

You see, the reason we all respond differently to the sermons we hear has more to do with our hearts than our ears. From a human perspective, how the Word of God impacts our lives depends on the preparedness of our hearts or, in agricultural terms, the condition of the ground. That's the point of the story that Jesus told about the sower, the seed, and the soils. This first parable,[1] best referred to as the "Story of the Soils," laid the foundation for all the other parables. In fact, Mark even went as far as to say that if you didn't understand this parable, you wouldn't be able to understand any of the others (4:13). And unlike many of the other parables Jesus would tell, He provided a clear and detailed interpretation/explanation of this parable. Jesus Christ is the sower ("the Son of Man"—Matt. 13:37—the one who preaches the Word). The seed is the Word of God (v. 11). And the soil on which the seed falls is the human heart (v. 12).

Agriculture was at the heart of Jewish life. It was the way they provided for themselves and made a living. Everyone understood the process of growing crops. The farmer would drape a bag of seeds over his shoulder and walk through the field throwing handfuls of seed onto the ground. It is likely that from where the crowd was sitting listening to Jesus tell this parable, they could actually see farmers sowing seed in the fields. And everyone understood that some of that seed was landing along the paths between the fields. Some was landing on top of rocks. Some was landing among weeds. And some was landing on fertile soil.

The fate of the seed—the yield of the seed—had everything to do with the condition of the soil.

Jesus used these four kinds of soil to illustrate four kinds of hearts on which the preached Word lands.

Some listeners have a stubborn, unreceptive heart.

Some listeners have a shallow, superficial heart.

Some listeners have a worldly, strangled heart.

Some listeners have the heart we all need if we are to respond properly to the Word of God: a soft, receptive heart.

Let's consider the four different heart responses to the preaching of God's Word.

THE HARD-PACKED PATH

The land of Palestine was covered with fields. There were no walls or fences. The only things that separated one field from another were paths. The dirt on these paths was packed down as hard as concrete from all the travelers. The seed that fell on the path could not penetrate the rock-hard soil. So it would get trampled underfoot, or birds would swoop down and eat it. This road soil represents the person with a heart that is hard and unreceptive toward God's Word. A lot of people in the world fit into this category. They are completely ignorant of and indifferent to the Word of God. The Bible and church are irrelevant to their lives. Some people with this kind of heart may show up at church from time to time and may even attend on a regular basis. But they couldn't care less about what is being said from the pulpit. They are disinterested, distracted, and bored with the preaching. The sermon goes in one ear and out the other. It bounces off their cold, hard heart like seed off asphalt.

The reason their heart is so hard that the Word cannot penetrate it is because it has been packed down by sin. Their heart has been trampled by an army of sinful thoughts and actions and words. They suppress the truth in their unrighteousness (Rom. 1:18) and have allowed their heart to be hardened by the deceitfulness of sin (Heb. 3:13). Therefore, their heart is totally unreceptive and unresponsive to the preaching of God's Word. Their heart shows no sorrow for their sin, no guilt, no true brokenness or repentance, and no concern for God and others. And Satan acts like a ravenous vulture hovering over their heart, waiting eagerly to pluck up the seed of God's Word as soon as it lands "so that they may not believe and be saved." Paul vividly described Satan's strategy for keeping people from experiencing salvation through Christ: "The god of this world has blinded the minds of the unbelieving, that they might not see the light of the gospel of the glory of Christ, who is the image of God" (2 Cor. 4:4). Does this describe your heart? Do you have a stubborn, unreceptive heart?

Interestingly, revealing the stony hearts of hardened listeners was part of the purpose of Jesus using parables to teach. While parables reveal truth to believers, they are equally effective at concealing truth from unbelievers. In between telling and interpreting this particular parable, Jesus said to His disciples, "To you it has been granted to know the mysteries of the kingdom of God, but to the rest it is in parables, so that seeing they may not see, and hearing they may not understand" (Lk 8:9–10; cf. Matthew 13:10–16). The mysteries of the kingdom refer to divine secrets that can be understood only by divine illumination. They are things you can't know on your own but that God has to reveal through parables. Jesus quoted Isaiah 6:9, where the nation of Israel had willfully rejected the words of the prophet and purposely closed their eyes and ears to the truth. They didn't want to see or hear the truth. So God obscured the truth and concealed it from them. Jesus was aware that there were people doing the same thing to Him as the Israelites had done to Isaiah. So He obscured the truth and concealed it from them as well. Often, the parables themselves were a punishment against unbelief, as the uncommitted spectators didn't have a clue what He was talking about and would never bother to ask Him to explain it. Instead, they rolled their eyes and walk away. But this also was by God's design. John Piper explains:

> Even when preaching the Word of God does not soften and save and heal, it is not necessarily ineffective. This preaching of the Word may be doing God's terrible work of judgment. It may be hardening people, and making their ears so dull that they will never want to hear again.... Don't be cavalier in the hearing of God's Word week after week. If it is not softening and saving and healing and bearing fruit, it is probably hardening and blinding and dulling.[2]

THE INCH-DEEP EARTH

This second soil is not referring to soil with rocks in it. Farmers would carefully cultivate their fields and remove the rocks. But in Israel, a layer of limestone runs through the land, and in some places it juts to the surface and only a few inches of topsoil cover it (Mark 4:5). The seed that landed on the shallow soil would begin to put down roots, but because the soil wasn't deep enough, the roots would hit the rock and the plant would have no place to grow but up. So it would grow up faster and produce more foliage than the rest of the crop. But it also wilted quicker because the roots could not get enough moisture, and it would shrivel up and die before producing any fruit.

The rocky soil pictures those who impulsively and enthusiastically respond to the Word of God without any thought of the cost. They embrace the gospel message with instant excitement but don't understand the significance of what it means to commit themselves to following Jesus Christ. They merely make a shallow, short-term commitment to Christ. Their faith is short-lived (Mark 4:17). As soon as they experience some sort of affliction or persecution for their professed faith in Christ, they punt their faith and end up leaving the church, which proves they were nothing more than "so-called brother[s]" (1 Cor. 5:11).

I know people like this. They have been some of my greatest disappointments in the ministry. They come running up after a message and tell me how wonderful it was and how convicted they are. They seem to be really broken about the way they have been living their lives. With tears in their eyes, they make a profession of faith in Christ. They are excited about reading their Bible and praying and coming to church. They speak out whenever they get a chance and even put some of the more mature Christians to shame with their zeal. They seem genuine. They look real. But as soon as they are required to take a stand or pay a price for being a Christian, the emotional high quickly fades away. As soon as the trials and temptations come, they fall back into their old lifestyle and they are never seen again. Conclusion: It was purely a temporary, emotional response. They are those described in 1 John 2:19 who "went out from us, but they were not really of us; for if they had been of us, they would have remained with us; but they went out, in order that it might be shown that they all are not us." Does this describe your heart? Do you have a shallow, superficial heart?

DEATH BY WEEDS

This third type of soil looked good on the surface, but below the surface was a vicious web of weeds and thistles just waiting to grow up around the plant. Weeds grow bigger and faster than plants. Their big leaves shade the plants from the sun, and their strong roots suck up all the moisture and leave none for the plant. As a result, the plant gets choked or strangled to death before it is able to produce any fruit (Matt. 13:22; Mark 4:7).

This soil describes a person who receives the Word but their heart and mind are so preoccupied with the things of the world that the gospel gets crowded out and choked to death. It doesn't die right away, but it gradually withers away. It dies a slow death.

Jesus describes three things that choke out the Word in a person's life. First are worries. These are the everyday cares and pressures of life like family, friends, school, work, finances, health, etc. These are the things that tend to cause anxiety in our hearts. Second are riches. This refers to all the material things in life including money, clothes, houses, cars, boats, Jet Skis, etc., that distract us from God. And third are desires. These are not just sinful desires like sex, drugs, and rock and roll, but also good desires like sports, academics, and hobbies that take time, energy, and money away from the Lord. These three things compete with Christ for our loyalty and affection, and too often Christ loses (Matt. 6:24–25; 1 Tim. 6:9–10; 1 John 2:15–16).

I see it happen all the time. Someone makes a profession of faith in Christ, but then some other person or thing becomes more important to them and Christ gets pushed aside. They start coming to church less and less and reading their Bible less and less and praying less and less and becoming less and less committed to Christ. All because they allowed themselves to get interested in the things of the world, then distracted, then preoccupied, then consumed, then obsessed, then choked, and finally, strangled to death by the things of the world. Demas is a tragic example of someone who chose the world over Christ (2 Tim. 4:10). Does this describe your heart? Do you have a worldly heart that is preoccupied with and strangled by the things of the world?

THE RIGHT SOIL FOR THE WORD

The good soil provides the perfect environment for seed to germinate and grow. It is soft, deep, and free of thorns and weeds. In it the seed flourishes and produces a bumper crop a hundred times more than was planted.

The good soil represents those who hear and understand and accept the preaching of God's Word (Matt. 13:23; Mark 4:20). They have an open, receptive heart toward the Word of God. Furthermore, they seek not only to understand what it means, but also strive to obey it, to put it into practice in their life. They are not just hearers of the Word but doers (James 1:22). As a result, the Word continually produces results in their life. They experience true, lasting change as a result of the sermons they listen to.

The presence of fruit is the only thing that sets the good soil apart from the other three soils in this parable. Every true Christian will consistently bear spiritual fruit in their lives (Matt. 7:16; Gal. 5:22–23). It is possible, however, for a Christian to backslide and fall away from Christ for a time. But if they are true believers, they will eventually come back to Christ and bear appropriate fruits of repentance (Matt. 3:8; Acts 26:20). There is no such thing as a fruitless Christian. Granted, not all Christians are as fruitful as others. The issue is not the amount of fruit in a person's life, but the presence of it. Jesus said, "My Father is glorified by this, that you bear much fruit, and so prove to be My disciples" (John 15:8). Does this describe your heart? Do you have a soft, receptive heart that produces the fruit of a true believer?

Immediately after the Parable of the Soils, Luke strategically placed another one of Jesus' parables, followed by a conversation Jesus had regarding the members of His family to emphasize the importance of listening to and obeying God's Word. Jesus described the fruitful life as a powerful light: "Now no one after lighting a lamp covers it over with a container, or puts it under a bed; but he puts it on a lampstand, so that those who come in may see the light. For nothing is hidden that will not become evident, nor anything secret that will not be known and come to light" (8:16–17).

In other words, the fruitful life is a witness to unbelievers (Matt. 5:16). Furthermore, Jesus explained that one day the condition of your heart will be revealed. He went on to say, "So take care how you listen; for whoever has, to him more shall be given; and whoever does not have, even what he thinks he has shall be taken away from him" (Luke 8:18). Even though Jesus changed the analogy from soil to light, it is obvious that this is the punch line of the entire passage. His point was that you need to be careful how you listen, because how you listen to God's Word determines whether you will be given more (good soil) or what you have will be taken away (road, rocky, thorny soil). In each case, what the first three soils thought they had was eventually taken away by the devil, trials, and the world.

All of it was taken anyway!

Luke concluded this section with the record of a conversation Jesus had with those who came to tell Him that His family had arrived: "And His mother and brothers came to Him, and they were unable to get to Him because of the crowd. And it was reported to Him, 'Your mother and Your brothers are standing outside, wishing to see You.' But He answered and said to them, 'My mother and My brothers are these who hear the word of God and do it'" (8:19–21).

In other words, the ultimate evidence that proves you are a Christian is that you hear and obey God's Word. This entire portion of Luke was designed to emphasize the importance Jesus placed on listening to the Word (vv. 8, 18, 21). Good soil yields the fruit of obedience from the Word of God. That fruitful life is a light that shines for all around to see, and it is the only real demonstration that you are spiritually identified with Jesus.

What kind of soil does the Word find when it falls on you? What kind of heart do you have for the Word of God?

FOR STUDY OR DISCUSSION

1. Read Psalm 95:6–11. How are the Israelites a classic example of the hard soil along the road? How does sin harden your heart and make it impenetrable to God's Word (cf. Heb. 3:12–13)?

2. Read Matthew 6:24–25; 1 Timothy 6:9–10; 1 John 2:15–16. What are some of the trials, temptations, persecutions, or worldly things that have or could potentially strangle your relationship with Christ?

3. Read Matthew 7:16–20 and John 15:8. According to Jesus, how do you distinguish a believer from an unbeliever? What evidence do you see in your life that proves you are truly saved?

Pray that God would cultivate in you a soft, humble, teachable heart in which the seed of His Word will sink deep down and grow up to produce much fruit in your life for His glory.

We are told men ought not to preach without preparation. Granted. But we add, men ought not to hear without preparation. Which, do you think needs the most preparation, the sower or the ground? I would have the sower come with clean hands, but I would have the ground well-plowed and harrowed, well-turned over, and the clods broken before the seed comes in. It seems to me that there is more preparation needed by the ground than by the sower, more by the hearer than by the preacher.

C. H. Spurgeon

Three

HARROWING YOUR HEART
TO HEAR

"Break up your fallow ground, and do not sow among thorns."

JEREMIAH 4:3

I f there is any encouragement to be found in Jesus' story of the soils, it lies in the fact that the soil can change. There is hope for the one who heeds Jesus' exhortation to "take care how you listen" (Luke 8:18). Our hard hearts can be softened. Our superficial hearts can be enriched and deepened. Our worldly, distracted hearts can be purified to receive afresh the Word of God.

As a boy growing up in New England, I spent many a summer day working in the garden. This was not your average-sized garden. It was so big that every spring my dad would get the farmer next door to bring in his tractor and plow to till up the soil. When he got done, there would be deep furrows and huge clods of dirt all over the garden. The farmer would hook up his harrow and drag it back and forth across the garden to smooth out the furrows and break up the clods of dirt so the garden would be level and ready for planting. Winter had taken its toll on the ground, but with the right effort, the earth could spring to life again.

In the Old Testament, God used this analogy to challenge the people of Israel to harrow up their hearts to make them ready to receive His Word. In Jeremiah 4:3, God said, "Break up your fallow ground, and do not sow among thorns." In Hosea 10:12, He said, "Break up your fallow ground, for it is time to seek the LORD until He comes to rain righteousness on you." Fallow ground referred to land that had been plowed but not seeded for one or more growing seasons, either to allow weeds to die or to make the soil richer. It was uncultivated, unused, and unproductive. As a result, it had become hard and useless. Before anything could be planted, it needed to be broken up and softened and made ready to receive the seed.

The exhortation "break up your fallow ground" summarizes the appeal made by the prophets of Israel throughout her history. The Israelites continually hardened their hearts in rebellion against God and His Word. They consistently failed to listen to what He told them to do and not to do. So He sent prophets like Jeremiah and Hosea to admonish them to harrow the soil of their hearts so they could receive His Word. If we are not careful, at times our hearts can get like that—hardened to God's Word. We may go through periods when we learn very little and change very little. That's when we know our hearts are in need of harrowing.

The writer of Hebrews warned us to be careful to not harden our hearts to the Word of God or allow our hearts to become hardened by the deceitfulness of sin. Quoting from Psalm 95, he wrote:

Therefore, just as the Holy Spirit says, "Today if you hear His voice, do not harden your hearts as when they provoked Me, as in the day of trial in the wilderness, where your fathers tried Me by testing Me, and saw My works for forty years. Therefore I was angry with this generation, and said, 'They always go astray in their heart, and they did not know My ways'; as I swore in My wrath, 'They shall not enter my rest.'" Take care, brethren, that there not be in any one of you an evil, unbelieving heart that falls away from the living God. But encourage one another day after day, as long as it is still called "Today," so that none of you will be hardened by the deceitfulness of sin. (Heb. 3:7–13)

During their wilderness wandering, the people of Israel repeatedly demonstrated a lack of faith in God and His Word. Even though they had seen countless examples of His marvelous provision and protection, they continued to murmur and complain and disobey what He said. As a result, God prohibited that rebellious generation from settling in the Promised Land and enjoying the blessings He had planned for them. When we disobey what God has said in His Word, we too forfeit divine blessings God intended for us to enjoy. When we hear the truth over and over again but fail to do anything about it, our heart grows harder and harder to the truth and eventually becomes completely insensitive to God's Word—no matter how many times it might be pricked by the Word of God, we are unfazed, just like when we poke a callus with a needle. The more we sin, the more calloused or hardened our heart becomes to God's Word. Sin deceives us and leads us away from God (Gen. 3:13; 2 Cor. 11:3), which makes our heart unprepared to hear His Word.

In this chapter, I want to suggest some things you can do to prepare your heart for the ministry of God's Word. These are the sharp discs of the harrow, designed to open your heart for the entrance of the Word that "gives light" (Ps. 119:130). A preacher's commitment to the Lord is to be prepared every week to stand and deliver His Word. Your commitment to the Lord should be to be prepared every week to sit and receive His Word. My goal is to be the best preacher possible. Your goal should be to be the best listener possible. When the preacher does his part and you do your part, God's Spirit will effectively use His Word to accomplish His purposes in your life.

READ AND MEDITATE ON GOD'S WORD EVERY DAY

Reading the Word on a daily basis will develop in you a healthy appetite for God's Word. You can't expect to come to church on Sunday with a hunger for God's Word if you haven't been feeding on it throughout the week. John Piper likens daily Bible reading to eating an appetizer that cultivates a spiritual appetite for the Sunday sermon; that is, it prepares and trains your palate for the main meal. If you have the privilege of sitting under a preacher who teaches through books of the Bible, the best hors d'oeuvre to get you ready to eat the main course on Sunday is to study the passage your pastor will be expositing next. Richard Baxter said, "Read and meditate on the Holy Scriptures much in private, and then you will be the better able to understand what is preached on it in public."[1]

This basic principle of meditation is clearly established in Psalm 1:1–3:

How blessed is the man who does not walk in the counsel of the wicked, nor stand in the path of sinners, nor sit in the seat of scoffers! But his delight is in the law of the LORD, and in His law he meditates day and night. He will be like a tree firmly planted by streams of water, which yields its fruit in its season and its leaf does not wither; and in whatever he does, he prospers.

Meditation serves as the bridge between interpretation and application, between knowing what a passage means and putting it into practice. To meditate means simply to think long and hard about the text—to mull it over and over again in your mind like a cow chewing its cud. Richard Baxter used this vivid analogy in describing what to do with a sermon after it is over: "Chew the cud, and call up all when you come home in secret, and by meditation preach it over to yourselves. If it were coldly delivered by the preacher, do you consider of the great weight of the matter, and preach it more earnestly over to your own hearts."[2]

Sometimes the application of a particular text of Scripture is crystal clear. Other times it takes a lot of time and effort before you see how a passage applies to your life. Asking yourself a series of questions as you meditate on a particular passage of Scripture will help you determine how it applies practically to your life. Based on 2 Timothy 3:16, which states that Scripture is useful for four things—"for teaching, for reproof, for correction, for training in righteousness"—start by asking yourself the following four questions every time you read the Bible:

- What did I learn ("teaching")?
- Where do I fall short ("reproof")?
- What do I need to do about it ("correction")?
- How can I make this a consistent part of my life ("training")?

When you pummel a passage with all these questions, at least one or more of them will likely pinpoint something you can apply to your life in a practical way. Then, when you are listening to the preaching of God's Word, your heart will be trained to apply these same questions to the text under consideration rather than having your mind wander throughout the sermon.

PRAY THROUGHOUT THE WEEK

First, you need to pray for yourself. You should pray that God would grant you an honest and good heart that would hear and accept the Word and that it will bear lasting fruit in your life, that He would make your heart soft and receptive to His Word, that your heart would delight in the truth of His Word more than in riches and food, that He would open your ears and help you to listen to and obey what He wants to say to you. Ask Him to speak to you in a very powerful and practical way, that He would cause you to change and grow to become more like Him. Ask Him to graciously illuminate your mind to understand what the Word means and how it applies to your life, that your heart would burn within you as the Scriptures are explained and that you would not be just a hearer of the Word but a doer of the Word. You must never forget that you cannot change all by yourself. You need God's help. Paul said to "work out your salvation with fear and trembling; for it is God who is at work in you, both to will and to work for His good pleasure" (Phil. 2:12–13). The author of Hebrews concluded his letter by reminding his readers that it is God who is "working in us that which is pleasing in His sight, through Jesus Christ, to whom be the glory forever and ever. Amen" (Heb. 13:21).

Second, you need to pray for the preacher. Pray that the preacher would preach with great liberty and boldness and clarity (Eph. 6:19–20; Col. 4:3–4); that God's Word would run rapidly, transforming people's lives for His glory (2 Thess. 3:1); that God's Spirit would empower the preacher and use him to help you grow in your understanding of God and His Word and accomplish His purposes in your life and the life of your church.

Philip G. Ryken writes:

> Most churchgoers assume that the sermon starts when the pastor opens his mouth on Sunday. However, listening to a sermon actually starts the week before. It starts when we pray for the minister, asking God to bless the time he spends studying the Bible as he prepares to preach. In addition to helping the preacher, our prayers create in us a sense of expectancy for the ministry of God's Word. This is one of the reasons that when it comes to preaching, congregations generally get what they pray for.[3]

Someone once asked Spurgeon the secret to the power and effectiveness of his preaching ministry. He replied simply, "My people pray for me!" During every sermon Spurgeon preached in his church, a large group of people was interceding on his behalf in the basement boiler room. This is just one of countless examples throughout church history where a congregation began to consistently and fervently pray for their preacher and his preaching was endowed with great power and revival broke out in the church and the community.

CONFESS YOUR SIN

Before you can ever receive the Word, you must get rid of sin in your life. James 1:21 says, "Therefore, putting aside all filthiness and *all* that remains of wickedness, in humility receive the word implanted, which is able to save your souls." The Word cannot even begin to sink in until you have cleaned house in your heart. Unconfessed sin and unreconciled relationships hinder your ability to hear and obey God's Word. It's like having wax in your ears that keeps you from hearing what God wants to say to you. You must be constantly dealing with the sin in your heart. That includes taking the initiative to make things right with any family member or fellow member of your church you have sinned against or has sinned against you (Matt. 5:23–24; 18:15–17).

Peter wrote, "Therefore, putting aside all malice and all deceit and hypocrisy and envy and all slander, like newborn babies, long for the pure milk of the word, so that by it you may grow in respect to salvation" (1 Peter 2:1–2). In order for us to truly long for God's Word and for God's Word to grow and change us into His likeness, we must first put off the sin in our life. This is essential if we are to be open and receptive to God's voice through His Word. Sin obstructs our ability to hear what God wants to say to us and impedes what He wants to do in us. That's why we need to make sure we come to church having confessed any known sin to God. Because in the same way sin hinders our communication to God through prayer (1 Pet. 3:7), so sin hinders God's communication to us through preaching. That means the clods of sin in our heart must be broken up and removed to make our hearts ready to receive the seed of God's Word. One of the simplest, most effective ways to prepare your heart for the preaching of God's Word is to spend some time on Saturday night or Sunday morning to prayerfully examine your life and humbly confess your sins to God. David's example of confession in Psalm 51 serves as a practical path to follow for getting your heart right before God.

REDUCE YOUR MEDIA INTAKE

According to the latest survey, the average American watches TV just over four hours a day. When you add in other media like radio, Internet, movies, and video games, the average daily media consumption is over nine and a half hours. The media saturation of our society has a dulling, deadening effect on our hearts. We are constantly being bombarded by visual stimulation, which conditions and diminishes our ability to listen to and comprehend the preaching of God's Word. In his textbook on public speaking, Duane Litfin points out that "Western society today is basically an eye-orientated rather than an ear-orientated culture...as this tendency to depend upon the eye has grown, our ability to listen has atrophied from disuse."[4]

This is the point of a recent book entitled *Preaching to Programmed People: Effective Communication in a Media-Saturated Society* by Timothy Turner. He explains how TV watching and preaching are diametrically opposed to one another—one is visual, the other is rational; one involves the eyes, the other involves the ears; one creates passive watchers, the other requires active hearers. Turner explains how TV fosters idleness and passivity by providing information that requires no response, whereas preaching seeks to generate some kind of change. If you are not careful, watching TV will turn you into a lazy listener who just sits there on the couch and takes in information and doesn't have to do anything with it. Typically people tune in to TV to tune out. They disengage their brain and expect to be entertained and amused. The fast-paced images and sound bites have shortened people's attention spans and created a passive spectator mentality where people are viewers rather than hearers and doers. After watching TV and going to the movies and surfing the Internet all week long, you come to church and have to sit and listen to a lengthy sermon that requires a great deal of concentration and exertion you aren't used to. You're expected to go from being a passive viewer to an aggressive listener literally overnight.

Listening demands a great deal of concentration and self-discipline. Augustine said, "To proclaim the Word of truth as well as to listen to it is hard work.... Thus, let us exert ourselves in listening."[5] Jay Adams writes, "Many today drift into church with their minds turned off, slouch in the pew, and expect the preacher to do the rest. Examine yourself, brother or sister: have you been guilty of becoming a Sunday morning version of the couch potato?"[6]

PLAN AHEAD, AND SCHEDULE YOUR WEEK AROUND THE MINISTRY OF THE WORD

For the majority of people, even church members, church is not the priority of their week. Too often school, work, sports, and other activities take precedence over going to church. They make the mistake of letting their time be ordered by the world, which views the weekends as a time to relax, to play sports, and to stay up late and sleep in. For Christians, however, Sunday should be the most important day of the week. You should try to schedule your work, activities, get-togethers, and vacations around church. You should live by the principle that Sunday morning starts Saturday night. Here are some practical suggestions on how to prioritize the Lord's Day:

- Make it a habit to be home on Saturday night.
- Be careful not to do, watch, or read anything that will cause lingering distractions in your mind the next day.
- Get things ready on Saturday night to alleviate the typical Sunday morning rush (lay out clothes, set the table, write the offering check, stock the diaper bag, etc.).
- Get a good night's sleep so you can be sharp and energetic to worship and serve God. It's hard to listen when you're nodding off.
- Eat a simple but adequate breakfast that will hold you until lunch. It's difficult to hear over the grumbling of your stomach.
- Work together with the other members of your family to get ready, and seek to establish and maintain a godly atmosphere on the way to church. Listen to music, sing, and pray together.
- Arrive at church ten minutes early instead of ten minutes late so you have enough time to find a parking spot, drop the kids off in the nursery or their Sunday school classes, get a cup of coffee, visit with your friends, and find a seat.

When you fail to plan ahead, Sunday morning ends up becoming a chaotic crisis, and by the time you get to church, you are frustrated and frazzled and your heart is in no condition to receive the Word. But when you plan well and are able to arrive in a relaxed, leisurely way, you will be in a much more receptive frame of mind.

BE CONSISTENT IN CHURCH ATTENDANCE

The author of Hebrews knew the dangers of sporadic worship and the inadequacy of that approach for the needs of the entire church: "Let us hold fast the confession of our hope without wavering, for He who promised is faithful; and let us consider how to stimulate one another to love and good deeds, not forsaking our own assembling together, as is the habit of some, but encouraging *one another*; and all the more as you see the day drawing near" (Heb. 10:23–25). David Eby expresses a common frustration of pastors. He writes:

> You grieve over flaky folks who don't take preaching very seriously, who will miss services with seemingly no conscience pangs, at almost any flimsy excuse. You mourn for a generation, red-eyed from Nintendo and TV, bloated with soccer, scouts, hot tubs, and designer vacations, but bored with the Word of God.[7]

Regular attendance in church is an aid to listening well, especially when your pastor is preaching through a book of the Bible or a special series. Patchy attendance breaks the continuity of a sermon series. Like skipping a chapter in a book or going to the restroom in the middle of a movie, you miss key information that is critical to understanding what is going on. If you have to miss church for some legitimate reason, it is always a good idea to get a CD copy of the message or download it on the Internet and listen to it so you can get up to speed and be on the same page with the rest of the study, along with everyone in your church.

GO TO CHURCH WITH A HUMBLE, TEACHABLE, EXPECTANT HEART

Come to church with a spirit of anticipation, fully expecting God to speak to you through His Word in ways that will make a lasting difference in your life. The psalmist expresses this longing in prayer: "Open my eyes, that I may behold wonderful things from Your law" (Ps. 119:18). It should be that you just can't wait to see what you're going to learn and how God is going to use His Word to convict you, correct you, comfort you, and change you. Jay Adams describes the manner in which we should approach the service:

> When you go to hear a sermon, you must be concerned about one thing: what does God have to say to me? Focus on God. See preaching as a transaction not merely between yourself and the preacher, but between yourself and God. The preacher is a means to that end. Go expecting to hear a Word from God that, when obeyed, will change your life.[8]

WORSHIP WITH ALL YOUR HEART

The most critical moments for the listener are those in and around and leading up to the sermon itself. You need to maximize this crucial time. Songs and prayers serve as a prelude to the preaching. The service is designed to set the table for the Word. The climax of the entire service is the sermon. You speak to God through the songs and prayers, and then He speaks to you through the sermon. Here are some suggestions:

- Sing enthusiastically, thinking about the words and considering them personal praises or requests.
- Follow along in your own Bible when the Scripture is read, taking note of the verses that most specifically apply to you.

- Listen attentively to the prayers that are prayed, and respond by affirming what you hear (saying "amen").
- During the sermon, follow along in your own Bible, turning to as many of the cross-references as you are able. God loves the sound of rustling pages as His children study His Word.
- Take notes. This is one of the simplest ways to increase the impact of a sermon on your life. It helps you stay focused, and it is more likely that you will remember the key points. Don't try to transcribe the entire sermon. Just write down the main points and the principles you most want to remember. This will serve as something tangible to take home and reflect on and discuss with others the truths taught in the sermon and how you plan to put them into practice in your life.

FIGHT OFF DISTRACTIONS

Who can forget the Lord's exhortation to Martha in all of her distraction? "Martha, Martha, you are worried and bothered about so many things" (Luke 10: 41)? Whenever the Word is preached, there is a spiritual battle going on. The last thing Satan wants is for you to hear the Word. So he does everything in his power to distract you and snatch away the Word from your heart and mind so it can't take root and grow and produce fruit in your life. Therefore, you must work hard at not being distracted, or worse, being a distraction to others.

I can still feel my mother's hot breath in my ear telling me that some people sitting behind us in church might end up going to hell if I didn't sit still. If I didn't stop squirming, she resorted to digging her long fingernails into my leg. Needless to say, I learned not to be a distraction in church. You can be a distraction by not turning off your cell phone or pager or by getting up and down to go to the bathroom. If you absolutely have to leave the service, when you come back, sit in the back or wait for a discreet moment to return to your seat.

Where you sit and whom you sit with play key roles in staying focused during the sermon. One of the easiest ways to remove a lot of the distractions is to sit up front, which puts most of the distractions behind you. Another helpful way to stay engaged is to be interactive. Don't just sit there like a pew potato. Show that you are being attentive by maintaining eye contact with the preacher, smiling, nodding your head, answering any rhetorical questions, quoting a verse along with the pastor, and saying "amen" when appropriate. What you say and do during the sermon impacts the preacher more than you will ever know. It disheartens a preacher when he sees you not paying attention, dozing off, whispering to the person next to you, getting up in the middle of the sermon, etc. On the other hand, when your body language and verbal affirmation show that you are fully engaged in the sermon, it spurs a preacher on, like a cheerleader cheering on an athlete from the sidelines.

The challenge with listening is that you can listen faster than a preacher can talk. The average listener can process over four hundred words per minute, whereas the average speaker is only able to say one-to two hundred words per minute. In light of the extra time your mind has while it waits for the speaker to catch up, you need to do everything you can to keep from dozing off or daydreaming about what's for lunch, who's playing today, or the big project due next week. If you have small children, utilize the nursery and children's church program. Not only will that keep your children from distracting those sitting around you, but it will also keep them from distracting you so you can listen without being constantly interrupted or overly concerned with what everyone else around you is thinking of your kids. What's more, by keeping your children with you in church, you may be inadvertently training them not to listen to the sermon when they grow up. Adams wisely points out:

> Thinking (wrongly) that it pleases God to drag children into
> pews before they are capable of understanding the preacher,
> parents teach their children to sit for 30–40 minutes, doing

something other than listening to the sermon. Some play with cars, dolls, or other toys. Others draw pictures or fold church bulletins into airplanes and hats. Many sleep.[9]

All these things teach kids to tune out during the sermon, which may be a difficult habit to unlearn later in life.

LISTEN WITH DILIGENT DISCERNMENT

The Bereans looked everything up in the Scriptures; so should you (Acts 17:11). God holds you personally responsible to determine whether or not what the preacher says is biblically accurate (Deut. 13:1–5; 1 John 4:1; 2 John 1:7–11). You need to think critically about what you are hearing. Don't just accept it because the preacher said it. Make sure what he's saying is what God has said. The Westminster Confession Larger Catechism states: "It is required of those that hear the Word preached that they attend upon it with diligence, preparation and prayer; examine: What they hear by the Scriptures; receive the truth with faith, love, meekness, and readiness of mind, as the Word of God; meditate, and confer of it; hide it in their hearts, and bring forth the fruit of it in their lives."

Whenever you listen to a sermon, don't critique it based on how creative or clever it is. It is the content of the sermon, not the delivery style, that matters most. Ask yourself whether the preacher interpreted and explained the verse or passage correctly, adequately supported his position from other places in the Bible, and practically applied it to your life.

PREPARATION OF THE HEART AND SOUL

I have been personally blessed by the preaching ministry of Alistair Begg. Every since the first time I heard him preach, I've been inspired by the power and conviction with which he preaches. When I was serving as a youth pastor, we had the privilege of having him speak to our student ministry. Afterward, as I walked him to his car, I asked him what the key to his powerful preaching was. I'll never forget his answer: "Martyn Lloyd-Jones said the key to powerful preaching is preparation; not just preparation of the sermon, but preparation of the heart and soul."

I'm convinced that this principle of preparation, particularly the preparation of the heart and soul, applies not only to those who are preachers but also to all those who listen to them. Just as the key to powerfully preaching God's Word is proper preparation of the heart and mind of the preacher, the key to being powerfully impacted by the preaching of God's Word is proper preparation of the heart and mind of the hearer. Even the most well-crafted, well-preached sermons will fail to change your life if they are not received by a well-cultivated, well-prepared heart.

FOR STUDY OR DISCUSSION

1. Read Ephesians 6:19–20; Colossians 4:2–4; and 2 Thessalonians 3:1. What specific things should you pray for the preacher? What potential impact could your prayers make on your pastor as well as on your church and community?

2. How has your media intake diminished your ability to listen to and live out biblical preaching? What is the difference between watching TV and hearing a sermon?

3. What tends to distract you from staying focused while listening to the sermon? What are some practical ways you can fight against those distractions?

Pray that God would help you do a better job
preparing your heart to receive God's Word,
and determine to make the most
of every opportunity you have to hear it.

Come to hear them, not out of curiosity, but from a sincere desire to know and do your duty. To enter His house merely to have our ears entertained, and not our hearts reformed, must certainly be highly displeasing to the Most High God, as well as unprofitable to ourselves.

George Whitfield

Four

THE ITCHING EAR EPIDEMIC

I solemnly charge you in the presence of God and of Christ Jesus,
who is to judge the living and the dead, and by His appearing
and His kingdom: preach the word; be ready in season and
out of season; reprove, rebuke, exhort, with great patience and
instruction. For the time will come when they will not endure
sound doctrine, but wanting to have their ears tickled, they will
accumulate for themselves teachers in accordance to their own
desires and will turn away their ears from the truth, and will turn
aside to myths.

2 TIMOTHY 4:1–4

I minister an hour away from what is said to be the largest, fastest-growing church in America. Every Saturday night and Sunday morning, thousands of people drive from all over our city to listen to a charming, polished communicator give positive, motivational talks. By his own admission, he purposely never mentions the word *sin* because God has called him to encourage people. Week after week, he says basically the same thing: "Stop thinking negative thoughts. Stop acting like you're a victim. Believe that God has good things in store for you. Discover the champion in you. You can become a better you!" It's nothing more than Norman Vincent Peale's power of positive thinking dressed up in

Christian language. Every time I've watched this pied piper preacher on TV, it sounds like he is giving the exact same message. And yet people are so bewitched that they keep coming back week after week. I've concluded it is because they like what they are hearing so much that they are willing to listen to the same basic "sermon" over and over again.

What is so misleading about this man's preaching is that every week before he begins his sermon, he gets everyone to hold up their Bibles and recite the following confession:

> This is my Bible. I am what it says I am; I have what it says I have; I can do what it says I can do. Today I'll be taught the Word of God. I boldly confess my mind is alert; my heart is receptive; I am about to receive the incorruptible, indestructible ever-living seed of the Word of God. I will never be the same. Never. Never. Never. I'll never be the same, in Jesus' name.

And yet God's Word is rarely ever taught from his pulpit. Even though everyone's Bible lies open on their laps during the entire sermon, he rarely refers to it. His sermons contain little or no biblical content, but they are very inspirational. We might say the hearts of these many multitudes of listeners are right. They are enthusiastically embracing the message, hanging on every word. The problem is, the message itself is unsound.

What's playing itself out at this ultra-megachurch, and many hundreds of others like it, is simply the principle of supply and demand. The demand creates the supply. The reason there is so much unsound teaching in the church today is because there are so many people who want to have their ears tickled. Church growth surveys show that people don't want to listen to long, technical sermons that focus on doctrine. They want to hear brief, chatty talks that address their "felt needs" (family issues, finances, relationships, anger, anxiety, depression, etc.). Many a preacher has gained a huge following by simply finding out what people want to hear and then repeating it week after week, and people come to listen in droves. It is natural to assume that a big church means God must be blessing the pastor for preaching the truth. But in light of the widespread itching ear epidemic that has infected the vast majority of churchgoers in our day, a large audience may be an indication that the preacher is simply telling people what they want to hear.

DIAGNOSING ITCHING EARS

The problem with modern-day preaching lies as much with those who sit in the pews as with those who stand in the pulpits. Listeners have forgotten what to listen for. They have lost their biblical discernment. No other passage in the Bible provides greater insight into the problem with listening today than 2 Timothy 4:1–4, the classic text in God's Word regarding the true, fundamental nature of preaching. These famous last words of the apostle Paul, written within weeks (maybe even days) of when he would be beheaded by the deranged Roman emperor Nero, show us how the importance of listening to the Word of God preached is based on the importance of the preaching of the Word of God.

The two are inextricably linked.

Joel Beeke notes that "John Calvin often instructed his congregation about rightly hearing the Word of God.... Calvin stressed proper hearing because of his high regard for preaching."[1] Calvin no doubt would affirm that an accurate understanding of how to properly listen to God's Word begins with and flows out of an accurate understanding of how God's Word is to be properly preached. Knowing his days were numbered, Paul put his pen to parchment for the last time, and with his dying breath, as it were, he wrote the following words to his beloved disciple Timothy:

> I solemnly charge you in the presence of God and of Christ Jesus, who is to judge the living and the dead, and by His appearing and His kingdom: preach the word; be ready in season and

out of season; reprove, rebuke, exhort, with great patience and instruction. (vv. 1–2)

In order to stress the gravity of this final charge and inspire Timothy to be faithful to obey it, Paul summoned God and Jesus Christ as witnesses to this epic occasion. He wanted to give Timothy the impression that he was standing before the throne of God in heaven, and both the Father and the Son were watching and listening to what Paul was commanding him to do. He wanted Timothy to realize that this was ultimately a divine order, mandated by God Himself.

If that wasn't enough pressure, Paul reminded Timothy that one day he would have to stand before God's appointed judge, His Son, the Lord Jesus Christ, and give an account of whether or not he had faithfully obeyed this charge. Paul was referring to the Bema Seat judgment, when every believer's acts of service will be reviewed and rewarded accordingly (Rom. 14:10–12; 1 Cor. 3:10–15; 2 Cor. 5:10). Those who serve as preachers and teachers of God's Word will undergo the strictest scrutiny and endure the severest judgment at the Bema Seat. James 3:1 says, "Let not many of you become teachers, my brethren, knowing that as such we shall incur a stricter judgment." Every preacher will be judged based on how he handled God's Word. That's why Paul had previously exhorted Timothy to "Be diligent to present yourself approved to God as a workman who does not need to be ashamed, handling accurately the word of truth" (2 Tim. 2:15). A desire for God's approval on the Judgment Day should be what ultimately motivates every preacher to faithfully preach God's Word.

Paul had just finished reminding Timothy in the previous chapter of how God's Word had powerfully impacted his own life and adequately equipped him to impact the lives of others as well. In 2 Timothy 3:15–17 Paul wrote:

From childhood you have known the sacred writings which are able to give you the wisdom that leads to salvation through faith which is in Christ Jesus. All Scripture is inspired by God and profitable for teaching, for reproof, for correction, for training in righteousness; that the man of God may be adequate, equipped for every good work.

In other words, Paul wanted Timothy to be absolutely convinced of the authority, ability, and adequacy of God's Word. His conviction regarding the divine character of Scripture was to compel him to preach it. A preacher's convictions about the Bible will be reflected in how he preaches. If he truly believes the Bible is the inspired, inerrant, infallible Word of God that is profitable for teaching, reproof, correction, and training in righteousness, then the Bible will serve as the sole source and subject of every sermon he preaches. He won't present his own ideas or opinions from the pulpit. He won't share his dreams and visions or other personal experiences. He won't just tell a bunch of jokes and stories. Why? Because he understands that there is nothing more important to say than what God has already said. In fact, he affirms that he has absolutely nothing to say apart from what the Bible says.

Biblical preaching is when what the preacher says comes directly from a verse or passage in the Bible. The meaning of the verse or passage is literally explained in its historical and grammatical context, and that meaning is creatively principalized into a timeless truth that relates to people's lives today. In other words, the preacher explains what the original author was saying to the original audience he was writing to and then shows how that original meaning applies to his present-day audience. This method of preaching is referred to as biblical exposition or "expository preaching."

Theologian Wayne Grudem provides an exceptional summary of expository preaching:

Throughout the history of the church the greatest preachers have been those who...have seen their task as being to explain the words of Scripture and apply them clearly to the lives of their hearers.... Essentially, they stood in the pulpit, pointed to the biblical text, and said in effect to the congregation, "This is what this verse means. Do you see that meaning here as well? Then you must believe it and obey it with all your heart, for God Himself, your Creator and your Lord, is saying this to you today!"[2]

That is the primary purpose of preaching—to teach people God's Word, so they can live the way God wants. If after listening to a sermon you do not have a better understanding of God's purpose for your life, then you have not heard biblical preaching. You may have received a few practical pointers about how to get along with your spouse, raise your kids, or manage your finances. You may have laughed and even cried and left feeling encouraged and motivated. But what you heard did not truly qualify as biblical preaching.

That's not to say the Bible was never referenced. But in the topical/textual style of preaching that has become so popular today, there is a tendency for verses to get skimmed over, or worse, ripped out of their context and used to make a good point but, unfortunately, not the point God intended. Too often, a verse or passage serves as nothing more than a launching point for the preacher to teach whatever he wants to teach. In churches where textual or "springboard" preaching is the norm, Bibles are faithfully carried and reverently read at the beginning of the sermon but then lay open on people's laps and are never referred to again. In churches where topical sermons are typical, few if any feel the need to bring their Bibles because they are never encouraged to use them since the verses mentioned in the sermon are conveniently displayed on a screen or some kind of fill-in-the-blank sheet in the bulletin.

But this doesn't seem to bother many churchgoers. In fact, if given the option between a systematic, verse-by-verse exposition of a book of the Bible or a more topical message where verses are plucked from all over Scripture and combined to create a special series on practical issues like marriage, parenting, sex, money, work, dating, stress, etc., most churchgoers would pick the topical series as their favorite because in their minds it is easier and more enjoyable to listen to and is seemingly more helpful to their everyday lives. This should come as no surprise since the charge Paul gave to Timothy was given with a view to the future when the church "will not endure sound doctrine, but wanting to have their ears tickled, they will accumulate for themselves teachers in accordance to their own desires; and will turn away their ears from the truth, and will turn aside to myths" (2 Tim. 4:3–4). We are living in that time period about which Paul warned Timothy.

There are lots of people in churches today who will not put up with sound, doctrinal preaching. They are intolerant of anyone who gets up behind a pulpit and preaches truth that confronts their sinful lifestyle or makes them feel uncomfortable. They flat-out refuse to sit there and listen. If they feel like the preacher is stepping on their toes, they either run him out of their church or find another church where the preacher strokes their ears and makes them leave church feeling good about themselves. They successfully insulate themselves from what they consider the offensive truths of the Bible by surrounding themselves with preachers who caress them rather than confront them, who tell them what they want to hear instead of what they need to hear. They evaluate preachers based not on whether their teaching lines up with the Scriptures, but on whether it tickles their fancies, scratches them where they itch, and satisfies their craving to always be encouraged and entertained. It seems most people these days prefer listening to light, uplifting, entertaining messages. If given the choice, they would rather hear fictional stories than biblical truths.

With so many turning a deaf ear to the truth, truth itself is fast becoming an endangered species within the evangelical church today. A little over one hundred years ago, C. H. Spurgeon was deeply concerned that the church in his day was drifting away from biblical truth. Spurgeon's sole passion was preaching the Word of God. He believed the church's tolerance for biblical preaching was beginning to wane. He saw other preachers compromising the Word of God and experimenting with alternative approaches and abbreviated messages. He believed the church was in great danger, likening it to a runaway train going downhill at breakneck speed. He felt compelled to boldly stand up and speak out against what he termed "the Downgrade." He said, "Everywhere is apathy. Nobody cares whether that which is preached is true or false. A sermon is a sermon whatever the subject; only the shorter it is the better."[3] Even though Spurgeon's words are over a hundred years old, they accurately describe what is going on in the evangelical church today.

John MacArthur, who in many ways is a modern-day Spurgeon and the leading advocate and model of expository preaching alive today, writes the following:

> There is a trend away from expository, doctrinal preaching and a movement toward an experience-centered, pragmatic, shallow, topical approach in the pulpit. Churchgoers are seen as consumers who have to be sold something they like. Pastors must preach what people want to hear rather than what God wants proclaimed.[4]

DEVELOPING DISCERNING EARS

Even if you have found your way to a good, solid church with a shepherd who faithfully feeds your soul with expositions of God's Word, it's important that you continue to develop a discerning ear. It is imperative that you learn to discern truth from error so you will not be led astray. Over and over again, the New Testament writers warned that the church would be inundated with all sorts of false teachers and false teachings that would seek to deceive people and lead them astray from the truth:

> "If anyone says to you, 'Behold, here is the Christ,' or 'There He is,' do not believe him. For false Christs and false prophets will

arise and will show great signs and wonders, so as to mislead, if possible, even the elect." (Matt. 24:23–24)

"I know that after my departure savage wolves will come in among you, not sparing the flock; and from among your own selves men will arise, speaking perverse things, to draw away the disciples after them. Therefore be on the alert." (Acts 20:29–31)

But false prophets also arose among the people, just as there will also be false teachers among you, who will secretly introduce destructive heresies, even denying the Master who bought them, bringing swift destruction upon themselves. Many will follow their sensuality, and because of them the way of the truth will be maligned; and in their greed they will exploit you with false words. (2 Pet. 2:1–3)

We are living in the times Jesus, Paul, and Peter predicted. The quantity and variety of false teaching within the church today is astounding. As part of this present generation, you are being exposed to more religious information and instruction than any other generation in the history of the world. You are constantly being bombarded by Christian TV, radio, books, magazines, videos, preachers, speakers, authors, conferences, seminars, etc., all of which claim to be teaching truths from the Bible. Sadly, the average Christian today is not equipped to sort through this spiritual smorgasbord of teachers and teachings and pick out what is true, right, healthy, and good for them and leave behind what is false, wrong, unhealthy, and bad for them.

BEING A GOOD BEREAN

The book of Job says, "For the ear tests words, as the palate tastes food. Let us choose for ourselves what is right; let us know among ourselves what is good" (34:3–4). Like a wine connoisseur who makes judgments between bad and good wines and good and better wines and better and best wines, we need to be like sermon-tasting connoisseurs who makes judgments between bad and good sermons, good and better sermons, and better and best sermons. If we fail to do this, we are easy prey for false teachers who intentionally disguise error to look like truth. The end result is lives filled with turmoil and confusion, as we are "tossed here and there by waves, and carried about by every wind of doctrine, by the trickery of men, by craftiness in deceitful scheming" (Eph. 4:14).

That's why it is critical that every listener learns to exercise discernment. Luke described the believers in Berea as "more noble-minded than those in Thessalonica, for they received the word with great eagerness, examining the Scriptures daily to see whether these things were so" (Acts 17:11). While many today might say they were being critical or judgmental, Luke commended the Bereans for wanting to make sure that what they were being taught was biblical. They wanted to know the truth because they loved the truth. So they checked to make sure that what the apostle Paul was saying matched up with the truth of God's Word. If the Bereans were screening the apostle Paul, who was speaking under the direct inspiration of the Holy Spirit, how much more should you screen what you hear in church, listen to on the radio, read in books, buy at the Christian bookstore, etc.?

MOVING FROM MILK TO MEAT

The spiritual discernment level within the church today is at an all-time low. It seems that fewer and fewer Christians have the desire or the ability to distinguish truth from error, right from wrong, good from evil. This is not a recent problem however. The writer of Hebrews confronted his readers for their lack of discernment in Hebrews 5:11–14. He wanted them to understand that a lack of spiritual discernment is a direct result of a lack of spiritual development (spiritual maturity). The two are linked together; they go hand in hand:

> Concerning him we have much to say, and it is hard to explain, since you have become dull of hearing. For though by this time you ought to be teachers, you have need again for someone to teach you the elementary principles of the oracles of God, and you have come to need milk and not solid food. For everyone who partakes only of milk is not accustomed to the word of righteousness, for he is an infant. But solid food is for the mature, who because of practice have their senses trained to discern good and evil.

The writer of Hebrews was addressing Jewish Christians in this passage, trying to show how the high priestly ministry of Jesus Christ, as foreshadowed by Melchizedek (Genesis 14), is far superior to the Levitical priesthood under which they had grown up. But he was concerned that what he wanted to teach them was way over their heads. They weren't ready for it. So like any good teacher who realizes his students aren't getting it, he interrupted his explanation and rebuked his readers for their spiritual immaturity. Even though his heart and mind were filled with all sorts of stuff he wanted to share with them, he could tell that they were not in the right spiritual condition to understand and appreciate what he had to say. Their spiritual immaturity kept him from being able to move forward with his teaching. In a similar way, Jesus said to His disciples, "I have many more things to say to you, but you cannot bear them now" (John 16:12).

The problem was not with the teacher or the material. The problem was with the readers. They had become dull of hearing. The phrase "dull of hearing" is a combination of two words: *no* and *push* ("no push"). In other words, they had no drive. They were slow learners, lethargic listeners, or literally "lazy-eared." Oftentimes, people say they don't like to go to church because the preaching is dull. What they don't realize is that they are the ones who are dull—dull of hearing. They might not have always been like that. The writer of Hebrews implied that his readers hadn't always been this way. Apparently their original eagerness to hear and respond to God's Word had cooled. Because of their own laziness and lethargy, they no longer listened carefully or thought critically and had gradually become spiritually dull toward the truth. They should have been much further along the path of spiritual maturity. Sufficient time had elapsed since their conversion for them to become well grounded in the faith. They should have been mature enough to pass on to others the truths they had learned over the years.

There seem to be a lot of people who have been Christians for many years but have never really grown spiritually. Some churches are guilty of stunting the growth of believers by either rehashing the gospel every Sunday or dumbing down their teaching to appeal to an audience of unbelievers. Since their focus is on entertaining the goats rather than feeding the sheep, believers are never trained and equipped to become mature disciples of Jesus Christ. Few ever seem to get past the basics. These Hebrew Christians, instead of being able to teach truth to others, needed to go back to kindergarten and have somebody teach them the ABCs all over again. Like babies, they were only capable of consuming the milk of the Word and were unable to digest the T-bone truths of the Bible.

Paul rebuked the Corinthians for the same thing:

> I, brethren, could not speak to you as to spiritual men, but as to men of flesh, as to infants in Christ. I gave you milk to drink, not solid food; for you were not yet able to receive it. Indeed, even now you are not yet able, for you are still fleshly. (1 Cor. 3:1–3)

Now there is nothing wrong with milk. It is good and necessary for the healthy growth and development of a newborn. It's normal to see a baby drinking a bottle. But if you are still rocking your teenager to sleep with a bottle, that's not normal, it's tragic. And yet many people who have been Christians for fifteen years or more are still drinking milk. That's not right. They should have graduated to eating solid food. The problem is they are unskilled and untrained in processing the deep truths of Scripture. They know the stories and can spout the verses, but they don't know how to practically apply them to the everyday issues and situations in their lives.

Here we come all the way back to the principle of supply and demand, where we began this chapter. Mature believers are able to eat and digest the prime rib principles of God's Word because they have sat under consistent expository preaching. As they feed on the meat of the Word, they grow spiritually mature, and with that comes growth in discernment. They want nothing to do with shallow, topical teaching, and they see right through the schemes of false teachers and their claims. John MacArthur writes, "No one can be truly discerning apart from the mastery of the Word of God. All the desire in the world cannot make you discerning if you don't study Scripture.... If you really want to be discerning, you must diligently study the Word of God."[5] As you develop a more thorough working knowledge of the Scriptures, you will grow in your ability to tell the difference between good and evil. You will no longer be like a baby who crawls around putting everything in their mouth simply because they lack the discernment to know what is clean and edible and what it dirty and unfit for human consumption. It is characteristic of a new believer to listen to any preacher, read any book, or go to any church and not be able to tell whether it is good or bad for them. But through disciplined study of God's Word, they will eventually develop the ability to discern good teaching from bad.

HOLDING FAST TO WHAT IS TRUE

Perhaps the most straightforward explanation of discernment in the Bible is found in 1 Thessalonians 5:21–22. Paul said, "But examine everything carefully; hold fast to that which is good; abstain from every form of evil." As Paul was wrapping up his letter to the saints in Thessalonica, he listed off a series of rapid-fire commands that outlined the essentials of the Christian life, the basic necessities to live as a Christian. The last of these commands was to exercise discernment. There are actually three commands involved in this overall command to be discerning. We are commanded to "examine," to "hold fast," and to "abstain." In order to become a discerning listener, you must be able to do these three things.

First of all, you need to carefully examine everything you hear (v. 21a). The opening conjunction "but" connects what Paul was about to say with what he just said. In verse 20, he commanded the Thessalonians to not "despise prophetic utterances." In the early days of the church, before the New Testament was completed, God gave certain men the gift of prophecy. They, along with the apostles, received direct revelation from God and communicated it to God's people for their edification, exhortation, and consolation (1 Cor. 14:3). These prophets were inspired by the Holy Spirit to speak and write exactly what God wanted them to, and it became the New Testament (2 Pet. 1:20–21). The inspiration of Scripture was still going on at the time Paul wrote this letter. God was still in the process of "breathing out" His revelation through certain men He had chosen for this sacred task. Consequently, Christians living in those days had to be able to distinguish between those who were truly inspired by God and those who were not.

It was common for some people to claim that they were prophets speaking for God. The believers needed a way to recognize who was telling the truth and who was lying. Along with the gift of prophecy came the gift of discernment, which was the ability to discern who was speaking for God and who wasn't (1 Cor. 12:10). The gift of discernment was given to keep the gift of prophecy in check the same way the gift of interpretation of tongues was given to keep the gift of tongues in check (14:26–29). All four of these gifts were temporary sign gifts given to the church in its infancy, and as the church grew and developed, these gifts ceased because they were no longer necessary, particularly when the canon of Scripture was completed.

An overall study of 1 and 2 Thessalonians reveals that some false prophets had come to Thessalonica and deceived and confused the local Christians about the Rapture and the Second Coming of Christ. Some people thought the "Day of the Lord" had already taken place. Others were concerned that those who had already died would miss out on the Second Coming. Apparently, some of the Thessalonian believers began to despise prophecies. They either treated them as unimportant or dismissed them altogether, which was the easiest way to avoid being deceived and confused by false teaching.

Paul, however, told them that they still needed to listen to prophecy because he did not want them to tune out what might very well be the Word of God. But, he said, as you listen, exercise discernment. Don't be gullible. Don't just blindly accept everything you hear. Carefully examine everything. The word for *examine* (Greek *dokimadzo*) means to judge, evaluate, or analyze something, to put it to the test for the purpose of approving or rejecting. This word was used of precious metals that were tested to see whether they were genuine. If they proved to be genuine, they were given a stamp of approval.

Like a jeweler who tests a diamond or gemstone to see if it is real or fake and who is able to spot imperfections and flaws, your job as a Christian is to test what you are taught to see if it is true or false and be able to spot any errors or half truths. Practically speaking, everything must pass three basic tests.

The Bible Test (Isa. 8:20; 1 Tim. 6:3; 2 Tim. 1:13)

The Bible is the ultimate standard by which we test everything. You must take whatever you see, read, hear, feel, and experience and make sure it matches up with what the Bible says. If it contradicts anything God has already said in His Word, then it isn't true—period. It's as simple as that.

The Spirit Test (John 16:13; 2 Tim. 1:14; 1 John 2:27)

God anointed you with the Holy Spirit to help you discern truth from error. The Holy Spirit illuminates your mind so that you are able to recognize God's Word when you hear it and detect and reject anything counterfeit.

The Jesus Test (1 John 4:1–3; 2 John 1:7–11)

The one thing most often distorted by false religions and false teachers is the doctrine of Christ. They either deny His deity, His humanity, His impeccability, His exclusivity, His miracles, His death and resurrection, or His second coming. You must make sure a group or individual's view of the person and work of Jesus Christ accurately reflects what the Bible teaches.

Once you determine whether something is true or false, right or wrong, good or evil, you need to do one of two things with it. If it is true, you need to "hold fast" to it (1 Thess. 5:21b). In other words, you must embrace it wholeheartedly and zealously protect it from any and every possible threat (2 Tim. 1:13; Titus 1:9; Jude 1:3). If it is false, you need to "abstain" from it (1 Thess. 5:22). To abstain from evil means to completely separate yourself from it and stay as far away as possible. Paul summarized these two opposing responses in Romans 12:9: "Abhor what is evil; cling to what is good." That is what it means to be a discerning listener. With your heart engaged and your mind trained to single out and savor only the pure truth of the Word, you may buck the trend of those flocking to the siren call of feel-good preaching.

FOR STUDY OR DISCUSSION

1. What evidences do you see in the church today that we are living in the age of the "itching ear" Paul prophesied about in 2 Timothy 4:3–4? Explain how the law of supply and demand works as it relates to false listeners and false teaching and how this has affected the spiritual health of the church.

2. Read Hebrews 5:11–14. With regards to your hearing habits, are you a lethargic listener or an energetic listener? a baby Christian or a mature Christian? a milk drinker or a meat eater? What are some practical ways you can train and develop your skills of discernment?
3. Read 1 Kings 3:9–12; Psalm 119:66; Proverbs 2:3–5; Philippians 1:9–10; James 1:5. What do these passages teach about the vital role prayer plays in developing discernment?

Cry out to God to grant you discernment
through your personal study
of His Word along with the sermons you hear from
discerning preachers and the conversations you
have with discerning believers.

Live under the clearest, distinct, convincing teaching that possibly you can procure. There is an unspeakable difference as to the edification of the hearers, between a judicious, clear, distinct, and skillful preacher, and one that is ignorant, confused, general, dry, and only scrapeth together a cento or mingle-mangle of some undigested saying to fill up the hour with.... Choose the most able, holy teacher that you can have, and be not indifferent whom you hear.

Richard Baxter

Five

THE DISCERNING LISTENER

As I urged you upon my departure for Macedonia, remain on at
Ephesus so that you may instruct certain men not to teach strange
doctrines, nor to pay attention to myths and endless genealogies, which
give rise to mere speculation rather than furthering the administration
of God which is by faith. But the goal of our instruction is love
from a pure heart and a good conscience and a sincere faith. For
some men, straying from these things, have turned aside to fruitless
discussion, wanting to be teachers of the Law, even though they do not
understand either what they are saying or the matters about which
they make confident assertions.

1 TIMOTHY 1:3–7

The Old Testament scribe Ezra is a hero of many preachers. His entire life was devoted to the ministry of the Word of God. As a scribe, he was responsible for copying it, memorizing it, modeling it, explaining it to the people, and exhorting them to obey it. For this reason, God's hand of blessing was uniquely on Ezra's life and ministry, as Ezra 7:9–10 states: "The good hand of his God was upon him. For Ezra had set his heart to study the law of the LORD and to practice it, and to teach His statutes and ordinances in Israel." In Nehemiah 8, Ezra was invited to dedicate the newly rebuilt walls around Jerusalem.

A crowd of about forty-two thousand people gathered together for this historic event. After spending close to two long, hard months rebuilding the walls, the people wanted to be refreshed with the Word of God. "Bring the book," they cried (v. 1). So Ezra, along with a select group of men, mounted a huge, high stage that had been custom built for this special occasion, and all the people rose to their feet in honor of God's Word. Then Ezra proceeded to "read from the book, from the law of God, translating [explaining] to give the sense so that they understood the reading" (v. 8). Ezra's expository ministry has served as a model for preachers down through the ages who have sought to help others better understand and apply the Scripture, and those gathered to hear the Word also serve as a great picture of God's design for listeners, ever demanding "the book."

In the New Testament, Jesus is the obvious model of the faithful shepherd-expositor. The gospels record how Jesus spent the majority of His time explaining and applying the Old Testament to His disciples and the masses. His sermons are excellent examples of biblical exposition (Matt. 5–7). His post-resurrection conversation with the disciples on the Emmaus Road provides the best illustration of expository preaching in the New Testament. Luke recorded, "Then beginning with Moses and with all the prophets, He explained to them the things concerning Himself in all the Scriptures" (24:27). When the two disciples later recognized it was Jesus who had spoken with them, they said to one another, "Were not our hearts burning within us while He was speaking to us on the road, while He was explaining the Scriptures to us?" (v. 32). Faithful, systematic exposition sets the hearts of ready listeners on fire.

The book of Acts documents how the apostles, imbued with the Holy Spirit, carried out Christ's commission and followed His pattern of ministry closely. From the sermons of Peter (Acts 2), Stephen (Acts 7), James (Acts 15), and Paul (Acts 17), it is clear that the apostles faithfully set themselves to explaining how God's promises in the Old Testament had been fulfilled in His death and resurrection, and therefore, people must repent and follow Jesus Christ as their Lord and Savior. Of all the apostles, Paul stands out as the premier model of faithful preaching. At his farewell visit with the elders of the Ephesian church, he reminded them of how diligently he had taught them the Word of God. He said, "I did not shrink from declaring to you anything that was profitable, and teaching you publicly and from house to house.... Declaring to you the whole purpose of God" (Acts 20:20, 27). Paul's statement seems to indicate that during his three-year stint in Ephesus, he systematically taught through the Scriptures in their entirety so the believers would know all that God wanted them to know so they could be all that God wanted them to be.

RAVENOUS WOLVES

These men furnish us with a rich and glorious picture of the type of ministry that we should seek out and support, but the Scriptures also provide us with mug shots of the types of teachers we should avoid and expose. They are the "certain men" Paul thoroughly warned Timothy about, those who "teach strange doctrines" (1 Tim. 1:3). Since the beginning of time, Satan has sought to shrewdly and subtly twist God's Word in order to lead people astray from the truth. It all started in the Garden of Eden when he deviously disguised himself as a serpent and craftily contradicted what God had told Adam and Eve. God had clearly commanded them to not eat from the tree of the knowledge of good and evil or else they would die. Satan tempted Eve, saying, "You surely will not die! For God knows that in the day you eat from it your eyes will be opened, and you will be like God, knowing good and evil" (Gen. 3:4–5). Eve listened to Satan's word rather than God's Word and plunged the human race into sin.

The apostle Paul provided the best commentary of Satan's original deception in one of the letters he wrote to the church in Corinth. He said, "But I am afraid that, as the serpent deceived Eve by his craftiness, your minds should be led astray from the simplicity and purity of devotion to Christ" (2 Cor. 11:3). Paul went on to warn the Corinthian believers about "false apostles, deceitful workers, disguising themselves as apostles of Christ. No wonder, for even Satan disguises himself as an angel of light. Therefore it is not surprising if his servants also disguise themselves as servants of righteousness" (vv. 13–15). Paul's warning was right in line with the warning that Jesus gave toward the end of the Sermon on the Mount. Jesus said, "Beware of the false prophets, who come to you in sheep's clothing, but inwardly are ravenous wolves" (Matt. 7:15). In other words, like their evil master Satan, the appearance of false teachers is deceiving. They disguise themselves as true shepherds, pastors, teachers, elders, and leaders in the church.

If a hungry, ferocious wolf jumps over the fence into a flock of sheep, all of them will notice and scatter. But if he walks through the gate impersonating a shepherd, it will be difficult for the sheep to tell it is a wolf. The only way the sheep can discern whether he is a shepherd or a wolf is by listening to his voice. Jesus said:

> "But he who enters by the door is a shepherd of the sheep. To him the doorkeeper opens, and the sheep hear his voice, and he calls his own sheep by name, and he leads them out. When he puts forth all his own he goes before them, and the sheep follow him because they know his voice. And a stranger they simply will not follow, but will flee from him, because they do not know the voice of strangers." (John 10:2–5)

As one of Christ's sheep, you need to have your ears trained to differentiate between the voice of a true shepherd and the voice of a stranger so you know who to flee from and who to follow after. You must be able to recognize wolves when you hear them since they are disguised as Christian preachers and teachers, Christian authors, Christian counselors, Christian singers, etc., who are being used by Satan to deceive and devour Christ's flock. It is both sad and scary that so many Christians today are naively following the voices of strangers and being led astray from the truth of God's Word.

In Paul's day, it was no different—savage wolves dressed like shepherds had slyly slipped into church leadership positions and were teaching things that were upsetting people's faith and turning them away from the truth. Paul urged Timothy to silence these false teachers by upholding the biblical truths they were seeking to undermine. In verses 3–11 of Paul's first letter to the young pastor Timothy, he explains how to sift them out. What's needed is a careful evaluation of the basis of their teaching, the result of their teaching, the focus of their teaching, and especially the gospel they are teaching. These are questions you can apply to any teacher you come across.

Is Their Teaching Based on the Word of God? Is It Consistent with What the Scripture Says?

Paul had originally planted the church in Ephesus during his second missionary journey. He spent close to three years there training and equipping this body of believers. While under house arrest in Rome, Paul wrote a letter to the church in Ephesus. He was later released for a short time and traveled around revisiting some of the key churches he had planted. When he arrived in Ephesus, he was grieved to find that the church had been overrun by false teachers, just as he had predicted in his final meeting with the Ephesian elders in Acts 20. After confronting the men who were teaching heresy, Paul traveled on to Macedonia, leaving behind his prized partner in ministry Timothy to oversee the reorganization process of the church and help it get back to the way God originally intended.

Apparently the demands and pressures were so overwhelming that Timothy was tempted to pack up and leave. Paul was writing to encourage him to hang in there and complete the daunting task he had entrusted to him. The main reason Paul wanted him to stay was to firmly deal with those who were teaching "strange doctrines" (Greek *heterodidaskalia*). This is the opposite of sound doctrine. It is false doctrine, teaching that distorts or misrepresents the truth of God's Word (error, deception, lies, heresy, etc.). It appears that Paul coined this term to describe teaching that was different from what had already been taught by Christ and the apostles. By that time there was a body of truth that was an agreed-upon standard by which all teaching could be tested or judged (Acts 2:42; Eph. 2:20; 1 Tim. 6:3; 2 Tim. 1:13). Today, the standard by which all teaching must be tested and judged is the sixty-six books of the Bible. If what a person teaches doesn't agree with what the Bible teaches, that person should be categorized as a false teacher. Simply stated, a false teacher is someone who teaches something different than what the Bible teaches.

It's not exactly clear what the false teachers in the Ephesian church were teaching. Paul indicated that they were preoccupied with silly side issues and loved to stir up debates over meaningless matters. They had a fascination with "myths and endless genealogies" that had no biblical basis whatsoever (1 Tim 1:4; cf. 2 Tim. 4:4; Titus 1:14). These kinds of things proliferated in rabbinical writings. Before the gospels were written, it was easy for heretics to make up stories about the life of Christ. For example, the Book of Thomas includes fictitious stories about Jesus' childhood, like how He would make sparrows out of clay and levitate kids who were being mean to others. Jews also had a keen interest in tracing their family tree back to their patriarchal roots (Titus 3:9). The Old Testament contains numerous lists of names. Apparently these false teachers added new names, embellished the stories, allegorized the meanings, and made them say things God never meant them to say. The source of all these myths and genealogies was human imagination rather than divine revelation.

It is all too common today for preachers and authors and singers to make confident assertions about certain things without ever giving any biblical basis for what they are saying. Much of what they say is based more on personal experience or professional research than on the Bible. When people integrate worldly ideas and personal opinions with Scripture, they unwittingly change the true meaning of Scripture. Some knowingly twist Scripture to make it say what they want it to say to serve their own ends. Others simply want to go deeper and go beyond the simple literal, historical, grammatical interpretation of Scripture and end up saying more than what Scripture says by claiming to have discovered something new, novel, and revolutionary. R. C. Sproul wisely writes:

> When we talk about understanding the content of a book that was completed 2000 years ago with the best minds in Western history having pored over the content of the texts, it is highly unlikely that we will come up with a radical, new insight that will change the whole dimension of understanding that book.[1]

A basic rule of thumb is if it sounds strange, it probably is strange. If you hear something you have never heard before, there is a good chance it came from some place other than the Bible. The best defense against being duped by false teachers is regular Bible study (1 Tim. 4:6). As you expose your mind to Scripture day after day, you will grow in your ability to discern truth from error. I've heard that the U.S. Treasury Department trains people to catch counterfeiters by having them study genuine bills so they become so familiar with the real thing that it is easy for them to spot a fake. Similarly, you should spend so much time studying and examining the truth of God's Word that error becomes easily noticeable to you.

Whenever you listen to a preacher or teacher, you need to ask yourself questions like: "What is the basis for their teaching?" "How do they know that?" "Where did they come up with that?" "On what are they basing their convictions or conclusions?" Even though it may sound good, if you can't find any verses to support what they are saying, then don't accept it.

Does Their Teaching Produce Growth in Godliness? Is It Unifying and Edifying to the Body of Christ?

We don't know for sure what these "myths and genealogies" were all about, but we do know that whatever they were they had no spiritual value whatsoever. They involved futile speculation that served only to stir up arguments and create factions within the church. They caused doubts in people's minds and produced more questions than answers. As a result, instead of establishing the Ephesian believers in their faith, these false teachers were upsetting their faith, and if left unchecked, they would end up ruining people's spiritual lives (2 Tim. 2:14, 16–18, 23; Titus 1:10–11; 3:9–11).

Rather than helping people have a clearer understanding of God's Word, false teachers confuse and frustrate people by merely speculating about things that the Bible isn't clear about or by spiritualizing the Scriptures to make them say something God never intended them to say. Don't have anything to do with preachers and teachers who focus on secondary, speculative issues that are pointless and fruitless and distract you from the truths that matter most. Whenever it sounds like a preacher or teacher is getting off track and wandering down a rabbit trail leading nowhere, you need to ask yourself, "So what's the point? What does this have to do with helping me grow and mature in my walk with Christ?" You don't have time for that kind of frivolous stuff. You need to devote your time and energy to studying and meditating on the great truths of the Christian faith that are foundational to building up your individual spiritual life and the spiritual life of the rest of the body of Christ.

The body of Christ, the church, is the primary tool God is using at this time to accomplish His purpose and plan of bringing people to repentance and faith in Jesus Christ and causing them to grow to become like Christ (Eph. 4:11–16). Futile speculations and fruitless discussions about secondary matters contribute nothing to the edification or building up of the church. In fact, they have the exact opposite effect; they tear it down. False teaching distracts and detracts from God's work. That's why Paul was so adamant that Timothy stay in Ephesus and shut up the false teachers. Otherwise, the Ephesian church would never experience the spiritual growth that sound doctrine produces in people's lives.

Paul went on to describe what true spiritual growth looks like. Unlike the false teachers, Paul's teaching had a specific purpose and a definite goal. Instead of leading nowhere, it led somewhere. It led people to greater godliness; that is, to be more like God. The ultimate aim of all biblical instruction is to help people live godly lives.

A godly life is characterized by several things. First is "love," an unconditional, sacrificial commitment to God and others (Mark 12:29–31). Love is the distinguishing mark of a Christian (John 13:35). The first thing sound doctrine produces in people's lives is a greater love for God and others.

The second thing it produces is "a pure heart." In the Bible, the heart represents the center of a person or the source of all their desires and decisions. To have a pure heart means that your inner life is not dirtied or stained with sin. This is a rich theme throughout the Bible. David wrote, "Who may ascend into the hill of the Lord? And who may stand in His holy place? He who has clean hands and a pure heart" (Ps. 24:3–4). Jesus said, "Blessed are the pure in heart, for they shall see God" (Matt. 5:8). Sound doctrine results in people living a more pure and holy life.

Third, sound doctrine produces "a good conscience." Your conscience is the God-given mental faculty that tells you what is right and wrong (Rom. 2:14–15). When you do something wrong, your conscience accuses and convicts you. It makes you feel guilty. On the other hand, when you do what is right, your conscience defends and affirms you. It grants you joy, peace, and confidence that you did the right thing. Sound doctrine teaches you what is right and wrong so that you can do the right things and maintain a clear conscience.

Finally, sound doctrine produces "a sincere faith," a faith without hypocrisy. The Greek word for *hypocrite* (Greek *hupocritos*) was used to describe an actor playing a part in a play. In one scene, he would wear a sad mask. In the next, he would wear a happy mask. A hypocrite, then, is a person who wears a mask. A phony and a fake. But someone who sits under sound doctrine develops genuine, sincere saving faith, just like it did in Timothy (2 Tim. 1:5). On the contrary, false teachers are a bunch of hypocrites. They are lovers of themselves, they have dirty and perverted hearts, their consciences have been seared and defiled, and they hold to an outward form of godliness rather than genuine, internal godliness (1 Tim. 4:2; 2 Tim. 3:2–5; Titus 1:12–16).

False teaching will not and cannot produce the godliness Paul described in this passage. In fact, it produces the exact opposite (2 Tim. 2:16–17). In describing false teachers, Paul wrote that they have "a morbid interest in controversial questions and disputes about words, out of which arise envy, strife, abusive language, evil suspicions, and constant friction" (1 Tim. 6:4–5). Paul listed five ungodly attitudes that result from false teaching. All of these words describe a complete breakdown in relationships. In other words, the result of false teaching is total chaos and confusion within the church. These are the deeds of the flesh, not the fruits of the Spirit (Gal. 5:19–23). Jesus said you would be able to know a false teacher "by their fruits" (Matt. 7:15ff).

In contrast, the fruit of sound doctrine produces strong, healthy, spiritually mature people whose lives are characterized by love, purity, integrity, and sincerity. This is what people who are regularly exposed to the clear, accurate teaching of God's Word look like. The test of all true teaching is whether it produces these qualities in people's lives. Ask yourself if what you are being taught is causing you to love God more, to be more loving toward others, to live a more holy and blameless life, and to be more genuine and sincere in your relationship with Christ. Bottom line: Does it help you live a more godly life?

Do They Humbly Seek to Honor God and Help Others? Is It Free of Charge and Free from Financial Appeal?

False teachers don't care about things like love, a pure heart, a good conscience, and sincere faith. Not only does their teaching not produce these things; it doesn't even try to. Rather than aiming at a target, they stray aimlessly in the wrong direction, like a lost traveler who never reaches his destination. Their messages are nothing more than idle, useless, empty dialogue and debate. They arrogantly and selfishly covet the preaching/teaching role within the church and yet lack the ability to teach. They are nothing more than self-centered know-it-alls who exude a confidence that would make you think that what they say is true, and yet they don't have a clue what they are talking about (2 Tim. 3:6–7).

False teachers are motivated by various impulses. For some it is to boost their egos. For others it is to build their bank accounts. Others are seeking recognition or wanting to satisfy their sensual lusts. They are not seeking to humbly honor God and help others. They are merely in it for themselves. They are selfish and conceited (1 Tim. 6:3–5; Titus 1:10–11).

From the beginning of time, there has been a long line of religious racketeers who prey on gullible people promising them help while taking away their money. From Balaam (2 Pet. 2:15–16; Jude 1:11), to Simon the Sorcerer (Acts 8:9–24), to Tetzel, who brazenly sold indulgences promising people that "every time a coin in the coiffure rings, a soul from purgatory springs," to many of today's televangelists who sit in opulent settings with expensive suits and lots of gold jewelry promising you the same kind of prosperity if you will just send them your "seed money." They justify their lavish lifestyle by saying it is God's blessing on their lives because of their great faith. They want you to believe you could be just like them if you would just trust God like they do.

One of the best ways to discern whether someone is worth listening to and learning from is to examine the focus of their teaching. Are they all about themselves or about money? Is their ministry focused on God's glory or their own glory? Do they appear to be indulging themselves at the expense of those they are supposed to be ministering? Are they constantly making financial appeals? Do they come across as prideful or humble?

What Is Their Gospel Message? Do They Explain It Clearly and Correctly? Is It Works-Based or God-Glorifying Grace?

Finally, you need to evaluate a preacher/teacher's gospel. Paul stated that these false teachers wanted to be "teachers of the law" (1 Tim. 1:7). But they misunderstood and misapplied the law. Nevertheless, that does not mean the law is bad. Paul clarified how the law and the gospel work together in perfect harmony. The law is God's will for humankind. It is the standard by which He wants us to live. It is summarized in the Ten Commandments.

It seems that these false teachers were mixing Judaism with Christianity and advocating some kind of works-based righteousness, teaching that a person can earn their salvation by keeping the law (doing good works). This is by far the most common heresy that has plagued the church since its beginning. It has taken many different forms, but it always comes down to saying that faith in Christ is not enough for salvation. You need to believe in Jesus Christ plus keep the sacraments or perform special rituals and ceremonies or be baptized or join a particular church or give a certain sum of money or do some other type of good work. And yet the Bible says over and over again that no one can earn salvation by doing good works. Salvation is a free gift of God's grace that we receive through faith alone in Christ alone (2 Tim. 1:9; Titus 2:11–14; 3:5, 8).

God did not give the law as a way for us to earn our salvation, by keeping the law. He gave the law to show us that we can't keep it and that none of us is good enough to save ourselves and that we desperately need a Savior. The purpose of the law is to expose our sinfulness and help us see how far we fall short of God's standard and how much we have offended a holy God so that we would flee in repentance and faith to Christ for salvation (Rom. 3:20; 7:7; Gal. 3:24).

Paul went on to give a lengthy list of the types of people the law was designed to expose: "lawless and rebellious, for the ungodly and sinners, for the unholy and profane, for those who kill their fathers or mothers, for murderers and immoral men and homosexuals and kidnappers and liars and perjurers" (1 Tim. 1:9–10). There is a clear connection to the Ten Commandments. The first three pairs in this list correspond to the first section of the Ten Commandments dealing with offenses toward God. Paul then goes on to list those who violate the second group of commands concerning our neighbor. He concludes with an all-inclusive reference to any behavior that is "contrary to sound teaching, according to the glorious gospel of the blessed God, with which I have been entrusted" (vv. 10–11), which is to say, any behavior that is in opposition to the pure, accurate, healthy teaching of God's Word or contradicts the gospel in any way.

Paul's measuring stick for what was true or false, right or wrong, was the gospel message God had entrusted to him. Paul warned the Galatians that "even if we, or an angel from heaven, should preach to you a gospel contrary to what we have preached to you, he is to be accursed!" (Gal. 1:8). He adamantly defended the gospel while at the same time affirming that there is no conflict between the law and the gospel. They serve equally important roles that complement each other. The law shows us that we are wretched sinners who deserve to die and go to hell, and the gospel shows us that Jesus died and rose again to provide forgiveness and eternal life to all who will repent and place their faith alone in Him for salvation. Simply stated, the law shows us *why* we need to be saved, and the gospel shows us *how* we can be saved.

So the fourth and final criterion for discerning whether or not someone is a true or false teacher is to evaluate their understanding of the harmony between the law and the gospel. The question you need to ask yourself is do they use the law properly as a preparation for the gospel message or as a means of salvation? Do they teach that a person can only be saved by grace alone through faith alone in Christ alone for God's glory alone?

I trust these simple, straightforward questions will help you be able to pick false teachers out of the line-up so you can turn a deaf ear to their unhealthy teaching and thus ensure you listen only to healthy, wholesome teaching that nourishes your soul and promotes your spiritual health and growth. Hearing sound doctrine on a consistent basis is vital. As John Stott explains, "It is plain throughout [Scripture] that the health of God's people depends on their attentiveness to His Word.... God quickens, feeds, inspires and guides His people by His Word.... That is why it is only by humble and obedient listening to His voice that the Church can grow into maturity."[2]

That's why you can't afford to be a passive listener. Your growth and maturity as a Christian are at stake. Improving your ability to discern biblical preaching when you hear it, along with your ability to apply what you hear to your life, will greatly increase the effectiveness of God's Word working in your life to grow and change you into who He wants you to be. I've noticed that those in our church who are growing the most in their walk with God and experiencing the most dramatic changes in their lives are the ones who are most receptive and responsive to the preaching of God's Word. In other words, the better listeners are becoming the better Christians. Why? Because they don't just hear the Word, but it becomes a part of their lives. They live out what they learn. They apply it. They put it into practice. That's what I want to talk about in the final chapter.

FOR STUDY OR DISCUSSION

1. Who are some false shepherds you recognize in the church today who are subtly twisting God's Word and leading people astray from the truth?
2. Compare 1 Timothy 1:5 with 1 Timothy 4:2; 6:3–5; 2 Timothy 2:16–17; 3:2–5; and Titus 1:12–16. What are some of the differences between what sound doctrine and false doctrine produces in a person's life?

3. How do the law and grace fit together in the gospel message? What is the main heresy to look out for in regards to how a preacher/teacher presents the gospel (Eph. 2:8–9)?

*Ask God to help you develop
the habit of carefully evaluating every teacher
you hear by asking the four simple questions
explained in this chapter.*

If you would hear the word aright, practice what you hear.... Hearing only will be no plea at the day of judgment—merely to say, "Lord, I have heard many sermons." God will say, "What fruits of obedience have ye brought forth?" The word preached is not only to inform you but reform you.... If you hear the word, and are not bettered by it...your hearing will increase your condemnation.... We pity such as know not where to hear; it will be worse with such as care not how they hear. To graceless disobedient hearers, every sermon will be a faggot to heat hell. It is sad to go loaded to hell with ordinances. Oh, beg the Spirit to make the word preached effectual! Ministers can but speak to the ear, the Spirit speaks to the heart.

Thomas Watson

Six

PRACTICE WHAT YOU HEAR

But everyone must be be quick to hear, slow to speak and slow to anger; for the anger of man does not achieve the righteousness of God. Therefore putting aside all filthiness and all that remains of wickedness, in humility receive the word implanted, which is able to save your souls. But prove yourselves doers of the word, and not merely hearers who delude themselves. For if anyone is a hearer of the word and not a doer, he is like a man who looks at his natural face in the mirror; for once he has looked at himself and gone away, he has immediately forgotten what kind of person he was. But one who looks intently at the perfect law, the law of liberty, and abides by it, not having become a forgetful hearer but an effectual doer, this man will be blessed in what he does.

JAMES 1:19–25

Alot of listeners are guilty of listening to preachers much like the people of Israel listened to the prophet Ezekiel. In Ezekiel 33:30–32, God said to Ezekiel:

"But as for you, son of man, your fellow citizens who talk about you by the walls and in the doorways of the houses, speak to one another, each to his brother, saying, 'Come now, and hear what the message is which comes forth from the LORD.' And they come to you as people come, and sit before you as My people, and hear your words, but they do not do them…. And behold, you are to them like a sensual song by one who has a beautiful voice and plays well on an instrument; for they hear your words, but they do not practice them."

Apparently Ezekiel was a very eloquent orator, perhaps not unlike your favorite radio preacher. The Israelites flocked to hear him preach just because they liked to listen to him, but they failed to do what he said. They were intrigued by his sermons but never obeyed a single one. They merely wanted to be entertained and had no intention of putting into practice what they heard. Herod and the Athenians were guilty of the same thing (Mark 6:21; Acts 17:21). Some of you may never miss a sermon, but you fail to put much of what you hear into practice in your life. As your mother might have put it, "it simply goes in one ear and out the other."

I'm sure you're familiar with the expression "practice what you preach." Those sitting in the pew count on the one standing behind the pulpit to live out what he says. There is nothing more hypocritical and dishonoring to God than when a preacher doesn't do what he tells his congregation to do. But it is just as hypocritical and dishonoring to God when a congregation doesn't do what the preacher tells them to do. As a preacher, I realize that people have every right to expect me to practice what I preach. But as a listener, you need to realize that a preacher has every right to expect you to practice what he preaches, that is to say, to practice what you hear.

While many in the church today lack discernment and are listening to bad preaching that is hurting them rather than helping them, perhaps many more are listening to good preaching that should be helping them. Week after week, good sermons fly by without ever penetrating their minds, piercing their hearts, and transforming them.

They experience very little growth and change in their lives. Why? It's because they imagine that listening is passive. According to Beeke, "True listening means applying the Word of God. If you do not practice the Word of God after you have heard it, you have not truly listened to God's message."[1] They are nonlistening listeners who have trained themselves to be impervious to the commands of God! And beyond that, they're missing the point. The great evangelist D. L. Moody used to say, "The Bible was not given to increase our knowledge but to change our lives."[2] In other words, preaching is simply a means to an end. The goal of preaching God's Word is transformation—people's lives changing and becoming more conformed to the image of Jesus Christ. Many of these nonlisteners are even convicted by Scripture, but they don't take the time to think through the specific ways their lives need to change as a result of what they have read or heard. Adams writes the following:

> They expect the preacher to do all the work for them. They expect him to apply the passage specifically to exact situations, answering all possible questions and suggesting various applications and implementations that pertain precisely to them. In other words, they expect him to do all the work. Selfishly, they forget that there are other people in the congregation and that the preacher cannot think solely of their particular circumstances.... To expect them [the listeners] to apply general principles to the particulars of their lives, however, is too much to ask. That's work![3]

Listening is hard work because application is inherent in it. You have to connect the information to your life, to do something about what you hear. Once you hear a sermon, the ball is in your court. Failure to apply a sermon is not just lazy listening; it is sin. James said, "To one who knows the right thing to do and does not do it, to him it is sin" (James 4:17).

WIDE OPEN FOR THE WORD

James was the leader of the church in Jerusalem. He was writing to Jewish Christians who had been forced to leave their homes and church in Jerusalem because of persecution. They were now scattered all over Asia and were experiencing all sorts of difficulties. Apparently word had gotten back to James that some of them weren't living out what they said they believed. James warned them that if what they said they believed made no difference in the way they lived their lives, they had what he called "dead faith," faith that is nothing more than a verbal profession or intellectual assent to the facts about Jesus and that has no power to save. With this concern in mind, James challenged them to examine their lives to make sure they had true saving faith.

In order to help them do this, he gave them a series of practical tests to determine the genuineness of their faith. The first test he gave them was their response to trials and temptations (James 1:2–18). In the opening verses of his letter, James explained how a true Christian responds to trials and temptations. The second test he gave them was their response to God's Word (vv. 19–25). In these verses, James explains how a true Christian responds to God's Word. If you want to experience a breakthrough in your listening life, understanding and applying this passage is critical.

First, James describes the receptive heart—the soil that's just right for the seed of the Word.

Be Utterly Teachable (vv. 19–20)

James started out by giving three rapid-fire commands: "Be quick to hear, slow to speak, and slow to anger." These commands seem to stand alone as three good pieces of advice. But the context tells us that they are not just general commands. They apply specifically to how we should respond to the Word of God. In the verse that comes immediately before these commands, James explained how we are regenerated "by the word of truth"

(v. 18). Immediately following these commands, James exhorted his readers to "receive the word implanted" and to "prove yourselves doers of the word" (vv. 21–22). So when it comes to God's Word, you should be quick to hear, slow to speak, and slow to anger. Each of these three demonstrates teachability.

To be "quick to hear" implies that you are eager to hear God's Word. You are an attentive, careful listener (Matt. 13:9; Luke. 8:18; Rev. 2:7). Someone has rightly said, "God gave us two ears and one mouth to remind us that we should listen twice as much as we speak." At the time James wrote this letter, Christians didn't have their own personal copy of the Scriptures. They depended on hearing it read and explained in public services. So it was imperative for them to pay careful attention when the Old Testament Scriptures were being expounded or when an apostle was preaching about Christ.

To be "slow to speak" means to not speak quickly or rashly. Don't be eager to share your own beliefs and opinions (James 3:1). God will hold you accountable on the Judgment Day for every careless word that comes out of your mouth (Matt. 12:36). That's why it is wise to be a person of few words (Prov. 10:19; 17:28). Ecclesiastes 5:1–2 says, "Guard your steps as you go to the house of God and draw near to listen rather than offer the sacrifice of fools; for they do not know they are doing evil. Do not be hasty in word or impulsive in thought to bring up a matter in the presence of God. For God is in heaven and you are on earth; therefore let your words be few."

In James's day, church services were a lot less structured. The people had the freedom to interrupt the preacher whenever they wanted to disagree or argue with him. James was exhorting his readers not to be so quick to debate with the preacher. After all, if the preacher is doing his job right and simply explaining God's Word and not his own ideas and opinions, then you are not debating the preacher, but God. James was cautioning them from arguing with God's Word. Homer Kent commented, "When eagerness to hear and heed God's Word is replaced by ambition to expound one's own ideas, bitter arguments can soon develop...those who are certain they are right must be cautioned against wrathful argument."[4]

To be "slow to anger" means to avoid allowing a deep-seated attitude of hostility or feeling of bitterness and resentment build up inside you in regards to God's Word. This phrase refers to "a disposition hostile to scriptural truth when it does not correspond to one's own convictions; manifested against those who faithfully teach the Word."[5] People have a tendency to get angry at God's Word when it confronts their sin or conflicts with a cherished personal belief or pattern of behavior. Typically their anger is directed toward the one who preached it to them.

King Ahab hated the prophet Micaiah because he never prophesied good concerning him. Even though he knew everyone else was just telling the king what he wanted to hear, Micaiah said, "As the LORD lives, what the LORD says to me, that I shall speak" (1 Kings 22:14). When Micaiah told the king he would die in the upcoming battle, Ahab angrily had him thrown into jail until he returned from battle. Ahab never made it back alive. When Jesus rebuked the people in His hometown for not embracing Him as the Messiah, they "were filled with rage as they heard these things; and they got up and drove Him out of the city, and led Him to the brow of the hill on which their city had been built, in order to throw Him down the cliff" (Luke 4:28–29). The Jews resented Stephen's sermon that pointedly exposed their sin, so they drove him out of town and stoned him to death (Acts 7:51–58).

Even believers, at times, can resent God's Word and the preacher who brings it. With a sarcastic tone, Paul asked the believers in Galatia, "So have I become your enemy by telling you the truth?" (Gal. 4:16). James was trying to defuse the residual resentment and hostility that plagued the believers to whom he wrote this letter. He told them the reason they should be slow to anger is because human anger, unlike righteous indignation that is directed toward sin, injustice, or heresy, is counterproductive to what God wants to do in our lives. God wants to produce His righteousness in you so you can live a life that is right in His eyes. Getting angry at His Word will keep this from ever happening. That's why it is imperative that you maintain an attitude of teachability whenever you listen to the preaching of God's Word.

Purify Your Heart (v. 21a)

The main command in verse 21 is to "receive the word." But according to James, before you can ever receive the word, you must first get rid of the sin in your life. The picture James painted is that of taking off a dirty outfit. This was one of Paul's favorite analogies to describe the sanctification process. In Ephesians 4:22 and 31, Paul said, "Lay aside the old self, which is being corrupted in accordance with the lusts of deceit.... Let all bitterness and wrath and anger and clamor and slander be put away from you." He said the same thing in Colossians 3:8, "But now you also, put them all aside: anger, wrath, malice, slander, and abusive speech from your mouth." Similarly, Peter wrote, "Therefore, putting aside all malice and all deceit and hypocrisy and envy and all slander, like newborn babies, long for the pure milk of the word, so that by it you may grow in respect to salvation" (1 Pet. 2:1–2).

While Paul and Peter listed specific sins that needed to be put off in order to be open and receptive to God's Word, James referred to sin generically as "filthiness." This was a medical term for earwax. Having sin in your life is like having wax in your ears that keeps you from hearing what God wants to say to you. James commanded his readers to get rid of the sin that remained in their heart. In order for you to be able to receive God's Word, you must be constantly cleaning sin from your heart. Purity is a prerequisite for receptivity.

Humble Yourself Before the Word (v. 21b)

Instead of responding angrily to God's Word (v. 19), James told his readers to receive the Word "in humility." This refers to a gentle and meek attitude that causes you to set aside your own preferences and opinions instead of stubbornly refusing to submit your will to God's Word. Receptivity to God's Word starts with a humble submission to the authority of God's Word. God told Isaiah, "But to this one I will look, to him who is humble and contrite of spirit, and who trembles at My word" (Isaiah 66:2).

Jeremiah Burroughs described this submission to his congregation:

> To have a congregation lie down under the Word of God which is preached to them is a most excellent thing.... God expects that you should submit your estates, your souls, your bodies, all that you are and have, to this Word. And that is another particular of the sanctifying of the name of God in hearing the Word, there must be a humble submission to it.[6]

There is nothing better for your souls than to lie down under the Word; to lay aside your pride and any resistance and let the surgeon of Scripture work as it will (Heb. 4:12).

Stott writes, "An essential element in Christian humility is the willingness to hear and receive God's Word. Perhaps the greatest of all our needs is to take our place again, humbly, quietly and expectantly at the feet of Jesus Christ, in order to listen attentively to His Word."[7] Mary serves as the model of one sitting at Jesus' feet quietly, humbly, and submissively "listening to His word" (Luke 10:39). Whenever you are listening to God's Word preached, you should have the same humble, submissive heart as young Samuel who, when he heard God calling his name, responded, "Speak, LORD, for Your servant is listening" (1 Sam. 3:10).

Show the Word Hospitality (v. 21c)

To be hospitable means to warmly and generously welcome a guest or to be friendly toward someone. James encouraged his readers to welcome the truth of God's Word with open arms. In other words, you shouldn't resist it, twist it, or argue with it. Simply accept what it says.

Again, the Thessalonians and Bereans serve as stellar examples of those who were extremely hospitable toward the preaching of God's Word (1 Thess. 2:13; Acts 17:11). James said that when you welcome the Word into your hearts, it's like a seed that takes root and begins to grow. The more you read God's Word, meditate on God's Word, and sit under the preaching of God's Word, the more your spiritual life flourishes and the more fruitful you will become as a Christian.

Know the Gravity of the Word (v. 21d)

James affirmed what is taught throughout the Bible, that the Scriptures are what God uses to save your soul (2 Tim. 3:15–17; 1 Pet. 1:23). Paul said, "God was well-pleased through the foolishness of the message preached to save those who believe" (1 Cor. 1:21). Of his own preaching ministry, Paul said, "For we are a fragrance of Christ to God among those who are being saved and among those who are perishing; to the one an aroma from death to death, to the other an aroma from life to life. And who is adequate for these things?" (2 Cor. 2:15–16). When Paul considered that the eternal destiny of the souls of his hearers hung in the balance whenever he was preaching, he was overwhelmed with his own inadequacy and the gravity of his task.

In his excellent book *The Supremacy of God in Preaching,* John Piper relates how this verse impacts him as he prepares to preach:

> You wake up on Sunday morning and you can smell the smoke of hell on one side and feel the crisp breezes of heaven on the other. You go to your study and look down at your pitiful manuscript, and you kneel down and cry, "God, this is so weak! Who do I think I am? What audacity to think that in three hours my words will be the odor of death to death and the fragrance of life to life! My God who is sufficient for these things!"[8]

If the gravity of the Word of God grips the preacher like this, how much more should it grip the hearer? When you realize that the eternal destiny of your soul is hanging in the balance every time you listen to the Word preached, you will respond to God's Word with great seriousness and attentiveness. Richard Baxter wrote:

> Remember that this God is instructing you, and warning you, and treating with you, about no less than the saving of your souls. Come therefore to hear as for your salvation. Can that heart be dull that well considereth, that it is heaven and hell that is the matter that God is treating him about?[9]

Understanding the gravity of God's Word is essential to being open and receptive to it.

So being receptive to the Word of God is marked by a willingness to receive it with a teachable, pure, humble, hospitable, and sober heart. Does this describe your heart when it comes to how you listen? Jay Adams writes:

> Christian, do you listen to preaching with a heart wide open to truth, a heart unprotected from thrusts of the Spirit's sword? Or is your heart hard, resistant to certain teaching? Have you so rationalized your sin that your conscience rarely, if ever, accuses you of certain sins anymore?... It is time to crack open those compartments of the heart that you have so successfully barred. Instead, bare them to the preaching of the Word. Listen with a willingness to hear, understand, apply, and obey. Until you do, preaching will be virtually valueless.[10]

LISTENING IS OBEYING

A proper response to God's Word begins by having an open, receptive heart. But it is not enough to just humbly and gladly accept the Word. You must act on it. You must be reactive to God's Word. A chemical reaction is when chemicals undergo a change. Perhaps you remember those high school chemistry experiments, when the test tube boils over after mixing two chemicals together. When you hear and receive God's Word, it should immediately elicit some kind of reaction. It should produce some kind of change in you.

There is an inseparable relationship in the Bible between listening and obeying. Throughout Scripture, listening is equated with obeying. In many passages, a direct connection is clearly made between listening and obeying (Exod. 15:26; Deut. 6:3–5; Luke 6:47; 8:21; 11:28). They are like two sides of the same coin. They are synonymous terms. In fact, there is a direct lexical link between the words "hear" and "obey" in both the Old and New Testament. The Old Testament word for "hear" is *sama*. This is the same Hebrew word used for "obey." There is no separate word for "obey" in the Old Testament. In the New Testament, the Greek word for "hear" is *akouw*. The word for "obey," *hupakouo*, which literally means "to hear under," is a derivative of the word for "hear." The implication is that, in God's mind, hearing and obeying are one in the same.

LISTENING IS LOVING

The Scriptures also make a direct connection between listening/obeying and loving. The main motivation to listen to and obey God's Word is love for God. In reiterating the law to the new generation of Israelites about to enter the Promised Land, Moses declared:

> "O Israel, you should listen and be careful to do it, that it may be well with you and that you may multiply greatly, just as the LORD, the God of your fathers, has promised you, in a land flowing with milk and honey. Hear, O Israel! The LORD is our God, the LORD is one! You shall love the LORD your God with all your heart and with all your soul and with all your might. These words, which I am commanding you today, shall be on your heart." (Deut. 6:3–6)

The Psalmist exuberantly exclaimed, "I love Your commandments" (119:127). In His farewell discourse to His disciples, Jesus said, "If you love Me, you will keep my commandments" (John 14:15). In other words, you should listen to God because you love Him. When you truly love someone, you long to please them by attentively listening to what they want you to do and then diligently doing it. It's the same with God. In fact, Dietrich Bonhoeffer said in his classic work *Life Together*, "Love to God begins with listening to his Word."[11]

Obedience to God's Word is one of the best proofs that a person genuinely knows and loves Christ as their personal Lord and Savior. The apostle John wrote, "And by this we know that we have come to know Him, if we keep His commandments. The one who says, 'I have come to know Him,' and does not keep His commandments, is a liar, and the truth is not in him; but whoever keeps His word, in him the love of God has truly been perfected" (1 John 2:3–5).

In his commentary on James, John MacArthur writes the following:

> If a profession of faith in Christ does not result in a changed life that hungers and thirsts for God's Word and desires to obey that Word, the profession is only that—a mere profession. Satan, of course, loves such professions, because they give church members the damning notion that they are saved when they are not. They still belong to Him, not to God.[12]

In a word, he is saying that many people are deceived. That is precisely what James was trying to help his readers avoid when he wrote to them saying, "Do not merely listen to the word, and so deceive yourselves. Do what it says" (1:22, NIV). This short statement summarizes the entire book of James. James was challenging his readers to examine their lives to make sure they weren't deceived into thinking they were Christians when they really weren't.

That's why James exhorted his readers to be the type of individuals who were in the habit of obeying God's Word and not just listening to it. Listening to God is not good enough. You must do what He says. The word *hearers* was used by the Greeks to describe someone who attended a lecture but was not a disciple of the lecturer. In our day, this would be equivalent to someone auditing a class. Those were my favorite classes in college because they were so easy. You could go to class and write down all the information, but you didn't have to do any homework or take any tests. I think some people attend church every Sunday like they are auditing a class. They take notes on the sermon and tell the preacher what a good sermon it was on the way out, but they never do anything with what they learn after they leave church. What they fail to realize is that the sermon actually starts after it is over. Joel Beeke writes, "A sermon is not over when the minister says 'Amen.' Rather that is when the true sermon begins. In an old Scottish story, a wife asked her husband if the sermon was done. 'No,' he replied. 'It has been said, but it has yet to be done.'"[13]

THE WORD IN THE MIRROR

One of the greatest compliments I've ever received was when someone said to me, "Pastor, I can tell that you really expect us to do what the Bible says!" That expectation is born out of a conviction that God didn't give us the Bible to merely analyze it and discuss its meaning. Knowing the meaning of a passage is only half of the Bible study process. The other half is applying that meaning to our lives. The job of a preacher is to explain what a passage means and then exhort his listeners to apply it to their lives. There's a story told of a preacher who assumed the pulpit duties at a new church and proceeded to preach the same sermon several weeks in a row. Eventually, some of the members of the church got frustrated and asked him why he kept preaching the exact same sermon every Sunday. He simply replied, "When you start living that one, I'll move on to the next one."[14]

If you are honest, you have to admit that you know far more than you are presently putting into practice. If you never heard another sermon, you would have enough biblical truth to work on applying for the rest of your life. You may feel spiritually satisfied by the fact that you go to church every Sunday, that you have your devotions every day, and that you go to Bible Study every week. But if you are not applying what you are reading and hearing, then you are only kidding yourself. You are forgetting the whole point of looking into God's Word in the first place.

James compared God's Word to a mirror. The purpose of a mirror is to show you what you look like so you can see what needs to be fixed, straightened, or changed. You may need to change your clothes, comb your hair, shave, put on makeup, etc. How foolish it would be for you to look in the mirror and see all the things you need to change and then simply shrug your shoulders and walk away without doing anything about what you saw, and worse, even forgetting what you saw. Yet that is exactly what you do whenever you walk away from reading your Bible or hearing a sermon but never do anything about what you read or heard. You are what James called a "forgetful hearer" (1:25).

Not only is this a foolish attitude to have concerning God's Word, but it is a dangerous one. When a person is constantly exposed to God's Word but doesn't respond properly to the truth they hear, they put themselves at risk of losing what truth they may already have (Matt. 13:10–13). If you don't plan on applying what you read, then don't waste your time reading the Bible. If you don't plan on acting on what you hear in church, then don't waste your time going. Not only are you just wasting your time, but more importantly you are heaping judgment upon yourself for neglecting the Word of God. Every time you hear the Word of God preached, you are training yourself to either obey or disobey God. The scariest thing about listening to God's Word without applying it is that your heart will eventually become hardened to it. It's been said that the same sun that melts butter hardens clay. There is no neutral ground with God's Word. Every time you are exposed to it, you are either being softened by it or hardened by it.

That's why you must be what James called an "effectual doer" (1:25), who is diligent to find ways and means to apply what you hear. Don't be lulled into thinking that a sermon is over when the preacher closes in prayer. Remember, that's when the real work begins. You must look intently into God's Word and carefully examine those areas in your life that it has shown you need to change. Just like a mirror, the Word of God never lies. It always tells the truth. It is brutally honest, and sometimes you won't like what it shows you about yourself. Nevertheless, you must be grateful for "the perfect law of liberty" (v. 25) that sets you free from slavery to sin and enables you to change and grow into the image of Jesus Christ. And when you change in obedience to God's Word, He promises to pour out His blessing on your life.

God encouraged Joshua with these words:

> This book of the law shall not depart from your mouth, but you shall meditate on it day and night, so that you may be careful to do according to all that is written in it; for then you will make your way prosperous, and then you will have success. (Josh. 1:8)

The Psalms begin with this promise:

> How blessed is the man who does not walk in the counsel of the wicked, nor stand in the path of sinners, nor sit in the seat of scoffers! But his delight is in the law of the LORD, and in His law he meditates day and night. He will be like a tree firmly planted by streams of water, which yields its fruit in its season and its leaf does not wither; and in whatever he does, he prospers. (1:1–3)

Jesus said, "Blessed are those who hear the Word of God and observe it" (Luke 11:28). He also said, "If you know these things, you are blessed if you do them" (John 13:17). These verses affirm the most elementary principle in God's Word. The bottom line of the Bible is this: If you obey God, He will bless you, but if you disobey God, He will curse you. Which would you rather be, blessed or cursed? It all depends on how careful you are to obey what God has said in His Word, not just some of what He said, or even most of what He said, but all of what He said.

God is most honored when your life lines up wholly with His Word and His Word is lived out practically in your life (Titus 2:5, 8, 10). Your life makes God and His Word look either good or bad. Nothing brings greater reproach on God and His Word than when those who profess to be Christians don't live according to the principles of God's Word. It causes people to conclude, "If that's what comes of going to church and hearing all those sermons from the Bible and going to all those Bible studies and reading the Bible every day, then I don't want anything to do with the Bible." But when others perceive that hearing and putting into practice biblical preaching has had a life-changing effect on you, that will pique their interest and give you an opportunity to share with them the truth of God's Word and how they too can honor God with their life (Matt. 5:16; 1 Pet. 2:12). In this way, good listeners multiply themselves, as the seed of the Word reaps a bountiful harvest.

Realizing that the reputation of God and His Word are at stake should provide all the incentive you need to carefully listen to and live out every sermon you hear so that your life accurately reflects what the Bible teaches. In the conclusion to a Sunday morning sermon on "Sanctifying the Name of God in Hearing the Word," Puritan pastor Jeremiah Burroughs gave this stirring exhortation to his congregation:

> I beseech you, brethren, in the name of Jesus Christ this morning that you who are hearers of the Word would glorify the Word, and glorify the name of God in the Word. Oh, that not one of you would be a disgrace or shame to the Word of God!... You should rather think thusly: "It would be better for me that I

should die, and that I were under the ground and rotting there, than that the Word of God should ever be disgraced by me...." If ever you have gotten any good by the Word, you should go away with this resolution: "I will labor all the days of my life to honor this Word of God that I have gotten so much good by." If this were but the resolution of every one of your hearts this morning, it would be a blessed morning's work.

If this was the resolution of everyone's heart after reading this book, I would consider it to be a blessed work

FOR STUDY OR DISCUSSION

1. What are some biblical truths you already know but are not putting into practice in your life? What is the most important truth you need to put into practice right now?

2. Read John 14:15; 15:14; 1 John 2:3–5? What is the greatest proof of the genuineness of a person's salvation? What proof is there in your life that you truly know and love God?

3. As you looked into the mirror of God's Word in this chapter, what was one thing in your life that you saw needs to change? What must you do to change? What is the first step you need to take? When and where will you start?

*Ask God to make you an effectual doer who is diligent
to find practical ways to apply His Word to the areas
in your life that need to change so that
you will experience His blessing on your life.*

You must give an account for every sermon you hear.... The judge to whom we must give an account is God...how should we observe every word preached, remembering the account! Let all this make us shake off distraction and drowsiness in hearing, and have our ears chained to the word.

Thomas Watson

Conclusion

LISTENING LIKE YOUR
LIFE DEPENDS ON IT

"Therefore everyone who hears these words of Mine and acts upon them, may be compared to a wise man, who built his house upon the rock. And the rain fell, and the floods came, and the winds blew and slammed against that house; and yet it did not fall, for it had been founded on the rock. And everyone who hears these words of Mine, and does not act upon them, will be like a foolish man, who built his house upon the sand. The rain fell, and the floods came, and the winds blew and slammed against that house; and it fell—and great was its fall."

MATTHEW 7:24–27

I t's seems important to end this book where it began—at the pulpit, the place designed by God to be the spark plug that ignites the gasoline of His Word in the lives of all who listen.

The main trend in preaching resources today seems to be on understanding and adapting to the changes in our culture that influence the way people listen to preaching. I have seen a dramatic increase in the number of contemporary books and journals on preaching that emphasize the importance of the preacher understanding who is listening to him. In order for preachers to communicate effectively in the twenty-first century, they need to know how to connect with an audience of postmodern listeners. Postmodern people have distinct needs and struggles that preachers need to be aware of so we can relate ideas to them in a way that is relevant to their lives. Pastors need to reinvent themselves, change their style of preaching to adapt to the postmodern cultural shift, and engage an inattentive society that is saturated by the media and suspicious of authority. The key is knowing who your listeners are and how the culture in which they live shapes the way they think and feel and hear sermons. It's all about relating to your listeners.

And sadly, preachers are redefining their own sacred task en masse to accommodate the felt needs of the postmoderns. Preaching must be less authoritative and more interactive. Don't presume to speak for God. Sermons should include more dialogue and less monologue. Pastors should be less confrontational and more conversational. As a result, an entire generation is being allowed to "accumulate for themselves teachers in accordance to their own desires" (2 Tim. 4:3).

But the truth is that while a pastor must be a student of culture, he is first and foremost a student of God's truth, which is relevant in any culture. As this book about biblical listening comes to conclusion, I want you to consider what's at stake in the matter, for preachers and for listeners.

Ask yourself, "What could possibly be more relevant than knowing that both those who preach and those who listen must give an account to Christ when He returns?" At the final judgment, the listeners will stand alongside the preachers and be held accountable for the part they played in the preaching of God's Word (2 Tim. 4:1–3). God's Word itself will be the solemn standard by which both preachers and hearers will be judged (John 12:47–48). While the preachers are judged by the sermons they preached, the listeners will be judged by the sermons they heard. Puritan preachers frequently exhorted their congregations to listen to their sermons in light of this looming liability they would all face someday. Richard Baxter wrote:

Remember that all these…sermons must be reviewed, and you must answer for all that you have heard, whether you heard it… with diligent attention or with carelessness; and the word which you hear shall judge you at the last day. Hear therefore as those that are going to judgment to give account of their hearing and obeying.[1]

David Clarkson stated:

At the day of judgment, an account of every sermon will be required, and of every truth in each sermon…. The books will be opened, all the sermons mentioned which you have heard, and a particular account required, why you imprisoned such a truth revealed, why you committed such a sin threatened, why neglected such duties enjoined…. Oh what a fearful account![2]

Therefore, whenever you sit under the preaching of God's Word, what should be in the forefront of your mind is that fearful day when you will be judged based on how receptive and responsive you were to what you heard. As was already stated in the first chapter of this book, what you do with what God has said in His Word determines not only what kind of life you have here on earth, but also where you will spend eternity. That is the bottom line of the Sermon on the Mount, which is arguably the greatest sermon ever preached (Matt. 5–7). Multitudes had gathered on the hillside overlooking the Sea of Galilee to listen to Jesus expound on how His followers were to live in a way that was radically different than everyone else in the world. Jesus concluded His famous sermon by calling on all those who were listening to act on what He told them. He challenged them to put into practice everything He had just preached.

In order to motivate the crowd to obey what He said, Jesus gave a closing illustration that contrasted two types of builders: a wise builder and a foolish builder. These two builders exemplify the two ways people respond to Christ's words. The wise builder represents those people who hear and obey His Word, and the foolish builder represents those people who hear but disobey His Word. All of us are in the process of building a house, that is to say, living our lives. We are all like one of these two builders. What kind of builder we are will determine how our life ends up. How we build has eternal consequences—it will lead to either eternal salvation or eternal damnation. Heaven and hell are on the line when it comes to listening to God's Word. The reality is that some of you reading this book will end up in heaven and some of you will end up in hell. Where you end up may very well be decided by what you do with what you have been taught in this book.

Before Jesus began His conclusion, He made a frightening statement that should convict the heart of everyone who claims Jesus as Savior and Lord. He said:

> "Not everyone who says to Me, 'Lord, Lord,' will enter the kingdom of heaven, but he who does the will of My Father who is in heaven will enter. Many will say to Me on that day, 'Lord, Lord, did we not prophesy in Your name, and in Your name cast out demons, and in Your name perform many miracles?' And then I will declare to them, 'I never knew you; depart from Me, you who practice lawlessness.'" (Matt. 7:21–23)

In my opinion, this is the most horrifying scene in the entire Bible. It is a picture of what is going to happen at the final judgment to people who think they are Christians but really aren't. These are not atheists or agnostics who are living in outright rebellion against God. These are religious people who believe in Jesus Christ, who live good, moral lives, who attend church every Sunday, who have been baptized, who take communion regularly, who are involved in ministry, who teach Sunday school, who sing in the choir, who may serve as an elder or deacon or may even be a pastor. Outwardly, they appear to be very committed to the things of God. But inwardly, they have never truly come to know Jesus Christ, and to their shock, He will banish them to hell for all eternity. This is the ultimate delusion—thinking you are going to heaven and then finding out after it is too late that you are going to hell.

According to Jesus, there are not just a few professing Christians who will experience this unexpected fate. He said there will be "many." A. W. Pink wrote:

> Never were there so many millions of nominal Christians on earth as there are today, and never was there such a small percentage of real ones.... We seriously doubt whether there has ever been a time in the history of this Christian era when there were such multitudes of deceived souls within the churches, who verily believe that all is well with their souls when in fact the wrath of God abideth on them.[3]

This is a strong warning to those who believe all the right things and do all the right things, thinking that is enough to get them into heaven. It's not about right beliefs or good works, but about living a life that is characterized by obedience to Jesus Christ. That's the only way you can be certain that you have truly come to know Him as your personal Lord and Savior. Everything else is just lip service, or "ear service" if you like.

Even as sinful human beings, we acknowledge that true commitment requires more than just words. It's not enough for me to tell my wife I'm committed to her. I need to prove it by the way I treat her. If I say, "I love you," but then treat her like trash, my words mean nothing. We know that a person can say anything they want, but what really matters is what they do. We say things like, "You're all talk, no action." Or, "Actions speak louder than words." We have a word for people who say one thing and do another. We call them hypocrites. In essence, Jesus was saying, "It's not what you say that matters, but what you do." You can say anything you want—you can even believe anything you want—but the ultimate proof that you truly know Christ is that you obey Him (John 3:36; 1 John 2:3–6; 3:7–10).

Jesus stressed this point by comparing those who hear His words and act on them with those who hear His words but don't act on them. Recall that James illustrated this same "hearing and doing" principle by describing two different ways of looking into a mirror. In this passage, Jesus illustrated the exact same principle by describing two different ways of building a house. In Palestine, there are lots of dry, sandy riverbeds that can be without water for months, even years. But then a sudden rainstorm will hit, and that dry creek bed is transformed into a raging river that has the power to sweep away everything in its path. In ancient Israel, flash floods were known to suddenly change course and wash away entire encampments, killing people and animals and destroying everything.

Wise builders understood the dangers of these flash floods and made sure to build their houses away from these washes and took the time to dig down deep until they found rock on which to build. It took a lot more time and energy to build on rock. They couldn't just slap up a house. But the hard work paid off because when the hurricane eventually hit, their house stayed intact despite the raging wind and rising floods.

In contrast to the wise builder, the foolish builder failed to take the future into account. He saw a nice sandy spot right in the middle of the streambed and said, "Who needs a foundation? It's not that important!" So he quickly slapped up his house. It looked just as good and felt just as safe and comfortable as the one the wise man had built up on the rock—until the hurricane hit. The house was completely wrecked. It was a total loss.

The storms Jesus was referring to in this analogy certainly apply to the trials all of us must face in life. Doers of the Word handle trials much better than those who are merely hearers of the Word. In fact, trials expose who the doers are and who the hearers are. Everybody looks the same when life is smooth sailing. But when the cancer diagnosis comes or the child rebels or the job is lost or the house forecloses, that's when the genuineness of a person's commitment to Christ is tested and revealed. That's when you see what your faith is really made of.

How you fare in the storms of life is the best indication of how you will fare in the final judgment. Ultimately, that is the storm Jesus was referring to here. Those who not only hear God's Word but also obey it will withstand the wrath of God and will enjoy eternal salvation in heaven. But those who merely hear what God's Word says but don't do anything about it will not survive the wrath of God and will experience eternal damnation in hell.

My wife and I were living in southern California when the Northridge earthquake hit in 1994. One of the things that fascinated me most was the random pattern of destruction. For months, streets were lined with debris from houses that had been destroyed. It was strange to drive down a street and see two houses right next door to one other—one in rubble but the other standing. Before the quake, both looked exactly the same; both seemed structurally sound. But the earthquake revealed a major difference. The houses that withstood the violent shaking were built on natural ground while the ones that were destroyed were built on fill dirt. It all came down to whether a house had a solid or loose foundation.

It's the same for your life. It all comes down to the kind of foundation on which your life is built. You may look the same as everyone else in your church. You may sing the same songs, hear the same sermons, go to the same small groups, serve in the same ministries, but when things all shake down in the end, some of you will be left standing in the righteousness of Christ, and some of you will be condemned to hell. The determining factor will be what is underneath the surface of your life. It's all about your foundation.

What is your foundation? Is your life built on the sinking sand of just *hearing* the Word, or is it built on the solid rock of *doing* the Word? This passage is a solemn warning that your eternal destiny will be determined by how you respond to God's Word. If you hear and obey God's Word, you will go to heaven. But if you hear and disobey God's Word, you will go to hell. What does your response to God's Word right now tell you about where you will spend eternity? In his sermon on "Hearing the Word," Puritan David Clarkson wrote:

> Hearing is the provision made for the soul's eternal well-being, its everlasting welfare depends on it; if you fail here, your souls perish without remedy. For salvation comes by faith and faith comes by hearing. It is an act of eternal consequence. According to our hearing, so shall the state of our souls be to eternity.[4]

In the end, it will all come down to what you did with what God has said in His Word. So listen to every sermon in light of eternity, because every sermon is truly a matter of life and death.

A QUICK-REFERENCE GUIDE
FOR LISTENERS

The following are some practical suggestions for individuals and families regarding your responsibility as a listener that will help you get the most out of the sermons you hear.

ANTICIPATION:
THE LISTENER'S RESPONSIBILITY
BEFORE THE WORD IS PREACHED

Spiritual Preparations

1. Spend time reading and meditating on God's Word every day (personal quiet time).
2. Men, lead your wife and children in regular times of worship throughout the week (family worship, Bible reading, prayer, and singing).
3. On Saturday night or Sunday morning, take time to get your heart ready for worship.
4. Read a portion of God's Word that focuses on worshipping God and/or personal cleansing from sin.
5. Thank God that through Christ you can come boldly into His presence to worship Him.
6. Seek God's forgiveness for any sins you have failed to confess and repent of during the week.
7. Express to God that you understand that your best, most fervent attempts at worship are nowhere near what He deserves,

and beg Him to help you worship Him wholeheartedly in spirit and in truth.

8. Plead with God to make your heart soft and receptive to His Word so that it will take root and grow up to bear lasting fruit in your life.

9. Ask God to graciously illuminate your mind to understand what the Word means and how it applies to your life and to cause you to be a doer and not just a hearer of the Word.

10. Pray for those who will be preaching/teaching God's Word, that His Spirit will empower them to speak clearly and boldly and be powerfully used by Him to accomplish His work in your life and in the life of your church.

11. Take the initiative to make things right with anyone you have sinned against or has sinned against you (your spouse, parents, children, brother, sister, fellow church member, etc.).

12. Come to church with a spirit of anticipation, fully expecting God to speak to you through His Word in ways that will change your life forever.

Physical Preparations

1. Make it a habit to be home on Saturday night (Sunday morning starts Saturday night).

2. Be careful not to do, watch, or read anything that will cause lingering distractions in your mind the next day.

3. Get things ready on Saturday night to alleviate the typical Sunday morning rush (lay out clothes, set the table, write offering check, prepare diaper bag, load car, etc.).

4. Get a good night's sleep so you can be sharp and energetic to worship God and listen to what He has to say to you.

5. Eat a good breakfast that will adequately hold you over until lunch.

6. Work hard at helping one another get ready.

7. Seek to establish and maintain a godly atmosphere on the way to church (listen to praise music, sing, pray, etc.).
8. Arrive at church ten minutes early instead of ten minutes late (plan ahead!).

We are told men ought not to preach without preparation. Granted. But we add, men ought not to hear without preparation. Which, do you think, needs the most preparation, the sower or the ground? I would have the sower come with clean hands, but I would have the ground well-plowed and harrowed, well-turned over, and the clods broken before the seed comes in. It seems to me that there is more preparation needed by the ground than by the sower, more by the hearer than by the preacher.

C. H. Spurgeon

ATTENTION:
THE LISTENER'S RESPONSIBILITY
WHILE THE WORD IS PREACHED

1. Greet one another warmly when you arrive at church.
2. Sit down a few minutes before the service starts, and spend a few moments in silent prayer to prepare your heart for what you are about to hear.
3. Follow along in your own Bible when the Scripture is read, taking special note of the verses that most apply to you.
4. Sing joyfully and enthusiastically, thinking about the words and considering them personal prayers of praise or petition.
5. Listen attentively to the prayers that are prayed, and respond by affirming what you hear with an appropriate "Amen."
6. Take notes during the sermon so you have something tangible to take home and reflect on. Write down the outline and any key principles and implications you want to remember.

7. Seek to encourage the preacher by your attentiveness while he
   is preaching (maintain eye contact, smile, nod your head, say
   "amen," etc.).

8. Fight off all distractions (concentrate, sit up front, etc.), and
   make sure you are not a distraction to others (talking, fidget-
   ing, getting up and down during the service, etc.).

9. Exercise discernment by making sure what the preacher says
   matches up with what God has said by comparing everything
   you hear to the Scriptures.

It is required of those that hear the Word preached that they attend upon
it with diligence, preparation and prayer; examine what they hear by the
scriptures; receive the truth with faith, love, meekness, and readiness
of mind, as the Word of God; meditate, and confer of it; hide it in their
hearts, and bring forth the fruit of it in their lives.

Westminster Confession Larger Catechism

APPLICATION:
THE LISTENER'S RESPONSIBILITY
AFTER THE WORD IS PREACHED

On the Lord's Day

1. After the service is over, let the preacher know specifically
   how the message encouraged or challenged you.

2. Get together with family and/or friends for lunch or in the
   afternoon or evening to discuss what you learned at church.
   Ask each other the following questions:
   - What was the Sunday school lesson/sermon about?
   - How did God speak to you personally?
   - How does your life need to change as a result of what you
     heard?

3. Spend time in prayer for one another.
4. Thank God for what He taught you from His Word.
5. Ask God to help you to live out what you learned.
6. Ask God to continue to work in the hearts of everyone who heard the Word that day (believers and unbelievers).

During the Week

1. Read over the verses covered in the sermon, along with your sermon notes, and mull over in your mind what you learned and how you plan to change. You may want to write out specific answers to these questions:
   * How does God want me to change (a specific belief, behavior, or attitude)?
   * What must I do to change?
   * What is the first step I must take to change?
   * Where and when will I begin?
2. Attend a small group with other like-minded believers who can provide the necessary encouragement and accountability to follow through with the changes you need to make in your life.
3. Begin preparing your heart in anticipation of the next sermon you will hear.

Congregations never honor God more than by reverently listening to His Word with full purpose of praising and obeying Him once they see what He has done…and what they are called to do.

J. I. Packer

ENDNOTES

Introduction

1. J. I. Packer, "Why Preach?" in *The Preacher and Preaching*, ed. by Samuel T. Logan Jr. (Phillipsburg: Presbyterian and Reformed, 1986), 28.
2. Doug Pagitt, *Preaching Re-Imagined* (Grand Rapids: Zondervan, 2005), 76.
3. Ibid., 214.
4. Sermon 28 from *The Works of the Reverend George Whitefield* published by E. and C. Dilly, London, 1771–1772. http://www.monergism.com/threshold/articles/onsite/howtolisten.html (accessed 21 April 2008).
5. Augustine in Jay E. Adams, *Be Careful How You Listen* (Birmingham, AL: Solid Ground Christian Books, 2007), 76.
6. J. I. Packer in *The Preacher and Preaching*, ed. Samuel T. Logan Jr. (Phillipsburg: Presbyterian and Reformed, 1986), 20.

Chapter 1

1. In case you're wondering, audiology is the science of hearing that originated out of the need to address the hearing damage in numerous World War II veterans. Audiologists specialize in diagnosing hearing problems and remedying them through hearing aids, implants, or surgery.
2. Assertion B. B. Warfield made in his classic work *The Inspiration and Authority of the Bible* (P & R Publishing, 1948).
3. This complete list of commands to listen and obey is like a line of concrete trucks that stretches as far as the eye can see and

serve to pour a theological foundation for listening and obeying:
Deut. 5:1; 6:3–4; 9:1; 12:28; 13:4; 20:3; 27:9; 32:1; Josh. 3:9; 1
Sam. 15:1, 1 Kings 22:19; 2 Kings 7:1; 20:16; 2 Chron. 18:18;
2 Chron. 20:15; Job. 37:2–5; 42:4; Ps. 34:11; 50:7; 81:8, 13;
95:6–8; Prov. 1:8; 2:2; 4:1, 20; 5:1, 7, 13; 7:24; 8:6, 32–33;
19:20; 22:17; 23:12, 19, 22; Ecc. 5:1; Isa 1:2, 10; 8:9; 28:14, 23;
32:9; 34:1; 39:5; 41:1; 42:23; 44:1; 46:3, 12; 48:1, 12, 14; 49:1;
51:1, 4, 7; 55:2–3; 66:4–5; Jer. 2:4; 5:21; 7:2; 10:1; 13:15; 17:20;
19:3; 21:11; 22:2, 29; 23:18; 28:7; 29:20; 31:10; 34:4; 44:24–26;
Ezek. 3:27; 6:3; 13:2; 16:35; 18:25; 20:47; 25:3; 33:30; 34:7–9;
36:1–4; 37:4; 40:4; 44:5; Hos. 4:1; 5:1; Joel 1:2; Amos 3:1; 4:1;
5:1; 8:4; Micah 1:2; 3:1, 9; 6:1–2; Zech. 3:8; Matt. 11:15; 13:9,
43; 17:5; 21:33; Mark 4:3, 9, 23–24; 7:14; Luke 8:8, 18; 9:44;
14:35; 16:29; Acts 2:14, 22; 7:2; 13:16; 22:1; Hebrews 3:7–8, 15;
4:7; James 1:19; 2:5; Rev. 2:7, 11, 17, 29; 3:6, 13, 22.

4. Thomas Shepard, "Of Ineffectual Hearing the Word," *The Works of Thomas Shepard* (New York: AMS Press, 1967), 3:366.

5. Old Testament examples of those who failed to listen and obey God's Word: Ex. 7:13, 22; 8:15, 19; 9:12; Deut. 1:43; 9:23–24; Josh. 5:6; Judg. 2:20–21; 1 Sam. 15:22–23; 1 Kings 20:36; 2 Kings 17:14, 40; 22:13; 2 Chron. 24:19; Neh. 9:16–17, 29–30; Ps. 81:11; 95:6–11; 106:25; Prov. 5:13; Isa. 1:2; 6:9–10; 30:9; 42:20; 48:8; 65:12; Jer. 5:21; 6:10, 17, 19 7:13, 24–27; 11:6–10; 13:10–17; 16:11–13; 17:23; 22:21; 25:3–9; 26:4–5; 29:19; 32:33; 34:14; 35:14–17; 36:31; 37:2; 40:3; 44:5–6, 16; Ezek. 2:5–7; 3:4–11; 12:2; 20:8; 33:31–32; Dan. 9:6; Zeph. 3:2; Zech. 1:4; 7:11–14.

6. John R. W. Stott, *The Contemporary Christian* (Downers Grove, IL: Intervarsity Press, 1992), 104.

7. Threats to those who failed to listen and obey God's Word: Lev. 26:14–27; Deut. 8:20; 9:23; 18:19; 28:15–68; 1 Sam. 12:15; Prov. 1:24–33; Isa. 66:4; Jer. 11:3; 12:17; 13:10–17; 16:11–13; 18:10; 19:15; 25:8–11; 26:2–6; 29:18–19; 35:14–17; 42:6–17;

Ezek. 20:34–39; Hos. 9:17; Mal. 2:2; Matt. 7:24–27; Luke 6:46–49; Acts 3:22–23.

8. New Testament examples of those who failed to listen and obey God's Word: Matt. 13:15; John 9:27; Acts 7:51, 57; 17:21; 28:26–27; Rom. 11:8; Heb. 5:11.

9. Promises of blessing to those who listen and obey God's Word: Ex. 15:26; 19:5–6; Deut. 7:12–16; 11:13–15, 26–28; 13:17–18; 15:4–6; 28:1–14; 30:11–16; 31:12–13; 1 Kings 11:38; Prov. 1:33; 8:34; 15:31–32; Jer. 7:22–23; 11:3–5; 18:10; Ezek. 20:39; Matt. 13:16; Luke 11:28; Rev. 1:3.

Chapter 2

1. One of the few parables that is recorded in all three of the Synoptic Gospels, the parable of the soils is also the first parable recorded by Matthew, Mark, and Luke, which implies that it was the first parable that Jesus ever told.

2. John Piper, "Take Care How You Listen," Pt. 1 & 2, delivered 22 February 1998, 6.

Chapter 3

1. Richard Baxter, *The Practical Works of Richard Baxter, Vol. 1, A Christian Directory* (Morgan, PA: Soli Deo Gloria, 1996), 473.

2. Ibid., 475.

3. Philip G. Ryken, "How to Listen to a Sermon." *www.tenth.org.* http://www.tenth.org/wowdir/wow2002-09-22.htm.

4. Duane Litfin, *Public Speaking: A Handbook for Christians* (Grand Rapids: Baker, 1992), 43.

5. Augustine in Jay E. Adams, *Be Careful How You Listen* (Birmingham, AL: Solid Ground Christian Books, 2007), 76.

6. Ibid., 51.

7. David Eby, *Power Preaching for Church Growth: The Role of Preaching in Growing Churches* (Ross-shire, Great Britain: Christian Focus Publications, 1996), 13.

8. *Be Careful How You Listen,* 40–42.

9. Ibid., 85–86.

Chapter 4

1. Joel R. Beeke, *The Family at Church: Listening to Sermons and Attending Prayer Meetings* (Grand Rapids: Reformation Heritage Books, 2004), 1.

2. Wayne Grudem, *Bible Doctrine: Essential Teachings of the Christian Faith* (Grand Rapids: Zondervan, 1999), 40.

3. John MacArthur Jr., *Ashamed of the Gospel: When the Church Becomes Like the World* (Wheaton: Crossway Books, 1993), xi.

4. John MacArthur Jr., *Our Sufficiency in Christ* (Dallas: Word Publishing, 1991), 134.

5. John MacArthur Jr., *Reckless Faith: When the Church Loses Its Will to Discern* (Wheaton: Crossway Books, 1994), 87–88.

Chapter 5

1. Eric J. Alexander, et al., *Feed My Sheep: A Passionate Plea for Preaching* (Morgan, PA: Soli Deo Gloria, 2002), 153, 155.

2. John R. W. Stott, *Between Two Worlds: The Art of Preaching in the Twentieth Century* (Grand Rapids: Eerdmans, 1982), 113, 133.

Chapter 6

1. Joel R. Beeke, *The Family at Church: Listening to Sermons and Attending Prayer Meetings* (Grand Rapids: Reformation Heritage Books, 2004), 17.

2. Richard Warren, *Twelve Dynamic Bible Study Methods* (Wheaton: Victor Books, 1981), 14.

3. Jay E. Adams, *Be Careful How You Listen* (Birmingham, AL: Solid Ground Christian Books, 2007), 49.

4. Homer A. Kent Jr., *Faith That Works: Studies in the Epistle of James* (Winona Lake, IN: BMH Books, 1986), 63.

5. John MacArthur Jr., *James* (Chicago: Moody Press, 1998), 72.

6. Jeremiah Burroughs, *Gospel Worship* (Ligonier, Penn: Soli Deo Gloria, 1990), 186.

7. John R. W. Stott, *The Contemporary Christian* (Downers Grove, IL: Intervarsity Press, 1992), 184.

8. John Piper, *The Supremacy of God in Preaching* (Grand Rapids: Baker, 1990), 37.

9. Richard Baxter, *The Practical Works of Richard Baxter, Vol. 1, A Christian Directory* (Morgan, PA: Soli Deo Gloria, 1996), 475.

10. *Be Careful How You Listen*, 59.

11. *The Contemporary Christian*, 109.

12. *James*, 77–79, 81, 84.

13. *The Family at Church*, 16.

14. Michael Fabarez, *Preaching That Changes Lives* (Nashville: Thomas Nelson, 2002), 184.

Conclusion

1. Richard Baxter, *The Practical Works of Richard Baxter, Vol. 1, A Christian Directory* (Morgan, PA: Soli Deo Gloria, 1996), 473–477.

2. David Clarkson, "Hearing the Word," *The Works of David Clarkson*, vol. 1 (Edinburgh: Banner of Truth Trust, 1988), 434.

3. James Montgomery Boice, *Matthew* (Grand Rapids: Baker, 2006), 259.

4. *The Works of David Clarkson*, vol. 1, 431.

BIBLIOGRAPHY

Adams, Jay E. *A Call for Discernment: Distinguishing Truth from Error in Today's Church.* Woodruff, SC: Timeless Texts, 1998.

———. *A Consumer's Guide to Preaching.* Wheaton: Victor Books, 1991.

———. *Be Careful How You Listen: How to Get the Most Out of a Sermon.* Birmingham, AL: Solid Ground Christian Books, 2007.

———. *Preaching with Purpose: The Urgent Task of Homiletics.* Grand Rapids: Zondervan, 1986.

———. *Truth Applied: Application in Preaching.* Grand Rapids: Zondervan, 1990.

Alexander, Eric J., et al. *Feed My Sheep: A Passionate Plea for Preaching.* Morgan, PA: Soli Deo Gloria, 2002.

Anyabwile, Thabiti. "1st Mark of a Healthy Church Member: Expositional Listening." *www.9marks.org.* http://www.9marks.org/partner/Article_Display_Page/0,,PTID314526_CHID775974_CIID2190814,00.html.

Azurdia, Arturo G. *Spirit Empowered Preaching: Involving the Holy Spirit in Your Ministry.* Ross-shire, Great Britain: Christian Focus Publications, 1998.

Baxter, Richard. *The Practical Works of Richard Baxter, Vol. 1, A Christian Directory.* Morgan, PA: Soli Deo Gloria, 1996.

Beeke, Joel R. *The Family at Church: Listening to Sermons and Attending Prayer Meetings.* Grand Rapids: Reformation Heritage Books, 2004.

Bickersteth, Edward. *The Christian Hearer.* Fleet-street, London: L. B. Seeley and Sons, 1828.

Boice, James Montgomery. *Matthew.* Grand Rapids: Baker, 2006.

———. *Whatever Happened to the Gospel of Grace?* Wheaton: Crossway Books, 2001.

Broadus, John A. *On the Preparation and Delivery of Sermons,* 4th ed., rev. by Vernon L. Stanfield. San Francisco: Harper Collins, 1979.

Burroughs, Jeremiah. *Gospel Worship.* Ligonier, Penn: Soli Deo Gloria, 1990.

Chapell, Bryan. *Christ-Centered Preaching: Redeeming the Expository Sermon.* Grand Rapids: Baker Books, 1994.

Clarkson, David. *The Works of David Clarkson*. vol. 1. Edinburgh: Banner of Truth Trust, 1988.

Craddock, Fred B. *As One Without Authority*. St. Louis, MO: Chalice Press, 2001.

Curtis, Gene E. "How to Teach People to Listen More Effectively to the Preaching or Teaching of God's Word." DMin dissertation, Gordon-Conwell Theological Seminary, 1999.

Dever, Mark. *Nine Marks of a Healthy Church*. Wheaton: Crossway Books, 2000.

Eby, David. *Power Preaching for Church Growth: The Role of Preaching in Growing Churches*. Ross-shire, Great Britain: Christian Focus Publications, 1996.

Fabarez, Michael. *Preaching That Changes Lives*. Nashville: Thomas Nelson, 2002.

Garrison, Webb B. *The Preacher and His Audience*. Westwood, NJ: Fleming H. Revell Company, 1954.

Graves, Mike, ed. *What's the Matter with Preaching Today*. Louisville, KY: Westminster John Knox Press, 2004.

Grudem, Wayne. *Bible Doctrine: Essential Teachings of the Christian Faith*. Grand Rapids: Zondervan, 1999.

Harris, Joshua. *Stop Dating the Church*. Sisters, OR: Multnomah Publishers, Inc., 2004.

Hendricks, Howard. *Teaching to Change Lives*. Sisters, OR: Multnomah, 1987.

Hendricks, Howard, and William D. Hendricks. *Living by the Book: The Art and Science of Reading the Bible*. Chicago: Moody Press, 1991.

Hughes, Jack. *Expository Preaching with Word Pictures*. Ross-shire, Great Britain: Christian Focus Publications, 2001.

Hughes, R. Kent, and Barbara Hughes. *Liberating Ministry from the Success Syndrome*. Wheaton: Tyndale, 1987.

Johnston, Graham. *Preaching to a Postmodern World: A Guide to Reaching Twenty-First-Century Listeners*. Grand Rapids: Baker Books, 2001.

Kaiser, Walter C. *Toward An Exegetical Theology: Biblical Exegesis for Preaching and Teaching*. Grand Rapids: Baker Books, 1981.

Kent, Homer A. Jr. *Faith That Works: Studies in the Epistle of James*. Winona Lake, IN: BMH Books, 1986.

Larsen, David L. *The Anatomy of Preaching: Identifying the Issues in Preaching Today*. Grand Rapids: Kregel Publications, 1989.

Lawson, Steven J. *Famine in the Land: A Passionate Call for Expository Preaching*. Chicago: Moody Publishers, 2003.

Liefeld, Walter. *New Testament Exposition*. Grand Rapids: Zondervan, 1984.

Leith, John. "Calvin's Doctrine of the Proclamation of the Word and Its Significance for Today in Light of Recent Research," *Review and Expositor* 86: 1989.

Litfin, Duane. *Public Speaking: A Handbook for Christians.* 2nd ed. Grand Rapids: Baker, 1992.

Lloyd-Jones, D. Martyn. *Preaching & Preachers.* Grand Rapids: Zondervan, 1971.

———. *The Puritans: Their Origins and Successors.* Edinburgh: Banner of Truth Trust, 1987.

Logan, Samuel T. Jr., ed., *The Preacher and Preaching: Reviving the Art in the Twentieth Century.* Phillipsburg: Presbyterian and Reformed, 1986.

Love, Christopher. *The Mortified Christian.* Morgan, PA: Soli Deo Gloria, 1998.

Lewis, Ralph L., and Gregg Lewis. *Inductive Preaching: Helping People Listen.* Westchester: Crossway Books, 1983.

MacArthur, John Jr. *Ashamed of the Gospel: When the Church Becomes Like the World.* Wheaton: Crossway Books, 1993.

———. *How to Get the Most from God's Word: An Everyday Guide to Enrich Your Study of the Bible.* Dallas: Word Publishing, 1997.

———. *James: Guidelines for a Happy Christian Life.* Chicago: Moody Press, 1986.

———. *Our Sufficiency in Christ.* Dallas: Word Publishing, 1991.

———. *Reckless Faith: When the Church Loses Its Will to Discern.* Wheaton: Crossway Books, 1994.

MacArthur, John Jr., Richard L. Mayhue, et al. *Rediscovering Expository Preaching: Balancing the Science and Art of Biblical Exposition.* Dallas: Word Publishing, 1992.

Mack, Wayne, and David Swavely. *Life in the Father's House: A Member's Guide to the Local Church.* Philipsburg, NJ: P & R Publishing, 1996.

Manton, Thomas. *The Complete Works of Thomas Manton.* vol. 15. London: James Nisbet, 1873.

Marcel, Pierre Charles. *The Relevance of Preaching.* Translated by Rob Roy McGregor. New York: Westminster, 2000.

Martin. A. N. *What's Wrong with Preaching Today?* Edinburgh: Banner of Truth Trust, 1992.

Mayhue, Richard. *How to Interpret the Bible for Yourself.* Ross-shire, Great Britain: Christian Focus Publications, 1997.

McQuoid, Stephen. *The Beginner's Guide to Expository Preaching.* Ross-shire, Great Britain: Christian Focus Publications, 2002.

Minkema, Kenneth P., ed. *The Works of Jonathan Edwards: Sermons and Discourses 1723–1729.* New Haven: Yale, 1997.

Mohler, R. Albert. *Preaching: The Centrality of Scripture.* Carlisle, PA: The Banner of Truth Trust, 2002.

Newton, John. *The Works of John Newton*. vol. 1. Edinburgh: Banner of Truth Trust, 1985.

O'Day, Gail R., and Thomas G. Long, eds. *Listening to the Word: Studies in Honor of Fred B. Craddock*. Nashville: Abingdon Press, 1993.

Old, Hughes Oliphant. *The Reading and Preaching of the Scriptures in the Worship of the Christian Church*. Grand Rapids: Eerdmans, 1998.

Olford, Stephen F., and David L. Olford. *Anointed Expository Preaching*. Nashville: Broadman and Holman, 1998.

Packer, James I. *A Quest for Godliness: The Puritan Vision of the Christian Life*. Wheaton: Crossway Books, 1990.

Pagitt, Doug. *Preaching Re-Imagined: The Role of the Sermon in Communities of Faith*. Grand Rapids: Zondervan, 2005.

Perkins, William. *The Art of Prophesying with the Calling of Ministry*. ed. Sinclair B. Ferguson. Edinburgh: Banner of Truth Trust, 1996.

Philip, William, ed. *The Practical Preacher*. Ross-shire, Great Britain: Christian Focus Publications, 2002.

Piper, John. *The Supremacy of God in Preaching*. Grand Rapids: Baker Books, 1990.

———. "Take Care How You Listen." Pt. 1 & 2, delivered 22 February 1998.

Postman, Neil. *Amusing Ourselves to Death*. New York: Viking Penguin, 1985.

Puritan Sermons 1659–1689. vols. 2 and 4. Wheaton: Richard Owen Roberts, 1981.

Robinson, Haddon W. *Biblical Preaching: The Development and Delivery of Expository Messages*. Grand Rapids: Baker Books, 1980.

Ryken, Philip G. "How to Listen to a Sermon." *www.tenth.org*. http://www.tenth.org/wowdir/wow2002-09-22.htm.

Scharf, Greg. *Prepared to Preach: God's Work and Ours in Proclaiming His Word*. Ross-shire, Great Britain: Christian Focus Publications, 2005.

Schlafer, David J. *Surviving the Sermon: A Guide to Preaching for Those Who Have to Listen*. Boston: Cowley Publications, 1992.

Schuringa, H. David. "Hearing the Word in a Visual Age: A Practical Theological Consideration of Preaching within the Contemporary Urge to Visualization." PhD diss., Theologische Universiteit van de Gereformeerde Kerkan, 1995.

Shepard, Thomas. *The Works of Thomas Shepard*. Vol. 3. New York: AMS Press, 1967.

Spring, Gardiner. *A Plea to Pray for Pastors*. Hoschton, GA: Shiloh Publications, 2000.

Spurgeon, Charles Haddon. *Lectures to My Students*. Ross-shire, Great Britain: Christian Focus Publications, 1998.

Steil, Lyman, Larry L. Barker, and Kittie W. Watson. *Effective Listening: Key to Your Success.* Reading, MA: Addison-Wesley, 1983.

Steil, Lyman, Joanne Summerfield, and George de Mare. *Listening: It Can Change Your Life.* New York: Wiley, 1983.

Stott, John R. W. *Between Two Worlds: The Art of Preaching in the Twentieth Century.* Grand Rapids: Eerdmans, 1982.

———. *The Contemporary Christian: Applying God's Word to Today's World.* Downers Grove, IL: Intervarsity Press, 1992.

———. *The Preacher's Portrait.* Grand Rapids: Eerdmans, 1961.

Stanley, Charles. *How to Listen to God.* Nashville: Thomas Nelson, 1985.

Sweazey, George E. *Preaching the Good News.* Englewood Cliffs, NJ: Prentice-Hall Inc., 1976.

Thomas, Curtis C. *Life in the Body of Christ: Privileges and Responsibilities in the Local Church.* Cape Coral, FL: Founders Press, 2006.

Thompson, William D. *Listening on Sunday for Sharing on Monday.* Valley Forge: Judson Press, 1983.

Turner, Timothy A. *Preaching to Programmed People: Effective Communication in a Media-Saturated Society.* Grand Rapids: Kregel Resources, 1995.

Veith, Gene. *Modern Reformation, Postmodern Times, www.modernreformation.com*: Sept-Oct 1995: 18–19.

Vines, Jerry, and Jim Shaddix. *Power in the Pulpit: How to Prepare and Deliver Expository Sermons.* Chicago: Moody Press, 1999.

Warren, Richard. *Twelve Dynamic Bible Study Methods.* Wheaton: Victor Books, 1981.

Watson, Thomas. *The Ten Commandments.* Edinburgh: Banner of Truth Trust, 1999.

Whitney, Donald S. *Spiritual Disciplines for the Christian Life.* Colorado Springs: Navpress, 1991.

———. *Spiritual Disciplines within the Church: Participating Fully in the Body of Christ.* Chicago: Moody Press, 1996.

———. "How to Make Every Sermon Count: Preparing Your Heart and Mind to Hear God's Word," *Discipleship* 106 (1998): 86–89.

Willhite, Keith. *Preaching with Relevance Without Dumbing Down.* Grand Rapids: Kregel, 2001.

Wolvin, Andrew and Carolyn Gwynn Coakley. *Listening.* 5th ed. Madison, WI: Brown & Benchmark Publishers, 1996.

Zink-Sawyer, Beverly. "The Word Purely Preached and Heard: The Listeners and the Homiletical Endeavor." *Interpretation* 51, no.4 (1997): 342–357.